To: Shirley

Thank you so much
for your prayers, love,
and support.

Doris Elaine Smart

07-31-2009

BEABO

The Robert Edward Johnston Story

His story of hurt, pain, and inability to forgive

by Doris Elaine Smarr

authorHOUSE®

AuthorHouse™
1663 Liberty Drive, Suite 200
Bloomington, IN 47403
www.authorhouse.com
Phone: 1-800-839-8640

First published by AuthorHouse 12/12/2008

ISBN: 978-1-4389-2824-1 (sc)
ISBN: 978-1-4389-2825-8 (hc)

Printed in the United States of America
Bloomington, Indiana

This book is printed on acid-free paper.

TABLE OF CONTENTS

DEDICATION

This book is dedicated to "Mama," Minnie House Smarr, the saint who raised me, loved me, protected me, educated me, encouraged me to reach for the stars, and most of all, taught me the word of God. Mama wore several hats; she was a minister's wife, a farm worker, and a nurse mid-wife. Mama raised three of her nine surviving grandchildren and gave unselfishly of herself to everyone.

To my son, Christian Ollemi (July 28, 1974–September 18, 1994). My son's love, compassion, bravery, and determination for life have left an indelible impression on my life. Christian was born with a learning disability but he was able in so many ways. There was nothing mechanical that he could not fix, and he was a very hard worker. I was so inspired by Christian and his spirit to never quit or give up on anything, and that was a contributing factor in my decision to write this book. I will always remember Christian's hardy laugh, the love and kindness he always showed, and I am eternally grateful to God for placing him in my life.

To my son, Kenny Ollemi: You are my heart. I thank you for all of your love and understanding when you had to sacrifice for your brother Christian, who needed a tremendous amount of care and attention. I know that there were times when you felt neglected and that time cannot be given back, but please know that you were always my favorite big man. You are a very precious treasure from God. I love you.

To Robert Edward Johnston, the man who helped inspire me to write his life story, I dedicate this book. Thank you for sharing your story with me. Your story reminded me so much of my son and his spirit never to give up, even when life seemed impossible. With each page my heart went out to you; I felt your every pain and ached for you. Your love of God, determination, spirit, and life has touched my heart in a way that can never be rivaled. Even though you have faced much turmoil in your life, you have never quit or given up. I will always remember you with all of God's love and caring. Without your consent and the valuable information that you shared with me, this story would not have been possible. I am proud of you and our friendship.

To all of the people who have supported and encouraged me to write this and other books with your love, loyalty, support, enthusiasm, and commitment. I am forever grateful to you, and I hope that this book will inspire you as it has inspired me to give your love unconditionally to everyone you meet, as this may be their story.

And to Amorite W. and Nellie G. Johnston, a poem of tribute from your adoptive son Robert E. Johnston.

WANTED

You took me from one that didn't want me
And gave me to, two that did
So in that union GOD created
A much loved and wanted kid

The house you brought me out of
Was filled with much despair
A love you normally find at home
Could never be found there

But where you took and placed me
Was warm and filled with love
Cause GOD you also lived there
Not just in Heaven, up above

The mom you chose was tender
And filled with warmth and love
The three of us a perfect fit
Just like a hand in glue

Mom taught me how to cook and clean
And she taught me how to sew
Mostly she taught about the love of GOD
Making sure his love I would know

The dad you placed into my life
Was big and oh so strong
He worked real hard and paid his bills
And did nobody wrong

(continues)

(continued)

The things my dad had taught me
Were good and very real
He taught me not to lie or cheat
And for GOD'S sake, do not steal!

Dad always taught me to forgive
And never hold a grudge
For if you do, you'll miss a chance
For friendship and true love

Life's lessons they did share with me
And material things they gave
So in the end and in return
I made sure that they were saved

By Robert E. Johnston
10-30-08

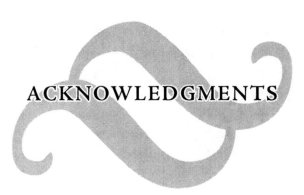

ACKNOWLEDGMENTS

Without your support, encouragement, and input, this book would not have been completed. I want to extend my heartfelt and sincere thanks to:

Aunt Janie Moore Brooks. You helped bring all of the facts together and made the project so much more interesting. Every family has a story to tell, and I learned a great deal of valuable information from you. I was amazed by your excellent memory at the age of eighty-eight.

Josie Brooks. Thank you for believing in me and encouraging me to complete this and other books and for checking on my progress daily. Your contribution of family pictures was greatly appreciated.

Jeanette Surratte. Thank you for providing me with pictures for the project and for your encouragement.

Harry Johnson. We all need a friend and mother like yours, who was willing to take in a homeless baby. Thank you for the road trip that you took to check on your best friend and brother. Your input has been very helpful and inspiring in completing this book.

Leonard Johnson. Thank you for your support of Harry and Robert.

Luther A. D. Ward III. Thank you for your valuable information and contribution to the success of this book.

Elijah Singleton. Good friends are hard to find, and when you have one that is as great as you are, you need to hold on tight. To the best friend and listener in the world, I thank you for the countless hours spent listening, advising, and encouraging. You are the greatest!

Regina Rauwolf Belcher. Thank you for taking your valuable time to read my first draft and give me encouragement to continue on.

My immediate family. You know me the best; you love me the most; and you have supported me in every way possible. I love you all very much.

Minister Mahalia Roberts. When I thought about slowing down or giving up, you were there, showing so much enthusiasm and constant encouragement.

Rev. William Thompson, Pastor. You are truly an anointed man of God and you have been such a blessing in my life. You have encouraged me with your ministry, words, and love. You have been more than a spiritual father to me.

AUTHOR'S NOTE

This book is a work of nonfiction. Some names and descriptions of individuals have been changed or omitted in order to protect their privacy. Some information may not be the exact word-for-word translation due to the passage of time, but the essence of the information is true to the best of my knowledge as it was related to me.

This is the Robert Edward Johnston story, and I will attempt to tell his story, in his own words, to the best of his recollection, as it was related to me.

Robert and I spent countless hours talking about his life and how much pain he continues to feel about his being abandoned as an infant.

Robert Edward Johnston, AKA Harold Felix Saucier, and I spent approximately three years together as friends, lovers, fiancées, acquaintances, and finally strangers.

I understand the pain and hurt that Robert has experienced, and I feel that same pain, but I also understand that unforgiveness and hatred are like cancers. At some point in one's life, we must be able to move beyond the past. You cannot walk backward into your future.

Moving beyond the past has been impossible for Robert, and it has literally destroyed his life.

Robert is a very bright and talented man. He is very intelligent, but has repeatedly focused his energy, knowledge, and intelligence in the wrong direction.

Everyone has a story to tell, whether good or tragic. This story is about my friend who had a tragic beginning, but I am praying to God for a miraculous end.

Some people can take a tragedy and turn it into a major victory, but others will permit it to defeat them in every way.

My friend has permitted his tragic life to defeat him in many ways; however, he has continued to fight to survive, even if in a negative manner.

His story was so compelling that I felt with all my heart that it needed to be told in order that it might help me, Robert, and others who may be in the same or similar situations.

I hope that Robert's story will be an inspiration to others in the same position to reach out to the people who take a chance to show them unconditional love.

PROLOGUE:
"ABANDONED"

Robert's Story Begins:

I believe that God has a plan for all of mankind, and I know that the plan is different for each and every one of us. I often question what God's plan could have possibly been for me, and I often question why I was born into this world.

I am not a rich man, not exactly a smart man; yes, I have made my share of mistakes, but I can't seem to give up on life and quit. What drives me? What does the future hold for me? Or is there a future for me?

I have so many questions because of my tragic beginning and the issues which I have had to face throughout my life.

Can you imagine being alive but not existing legally? I have so many questions for which there appear to be no answers. Why? Why? Why? Why was I chosen to live my life in so much pain and fear? I just couldn't seem to get through the hurt and pain even though I knew that I was blessed to be here and alive. My mother could have aborted me; why didn't she? She could have murdered me later on; why didn't she? She could have kept me and loved me; why didn't she? I guess that I will never know the answer to these questions because the one person who could have answered them honestly from her heart is now deceased. It leaves me only to ponder and question my existence.

I was now fifty-seven years old and did not know who I was or where I belonged. I mean this literally: I do not have a name or a true identity.

I have a Delayed Record of Birth, which was recorded on March 5, 1974, when I was twenty-two years old. I had no knowledge of this record until it was acquired for me by a dear friend in the year 2006. The birth record that was recorded in 1974 is for a Harold Felix Saucier, but there is no record for the birth of Robert Edward Johnston.

To understand my dilemma, you must know my story in its entirety; I will attempt to tell it to the best of my knowledge and understanding.

According to the information given to me by Amorite W. and Nellie G. Brooks Johnston, the couple who raised me from a young child, I was born on June 22, 1951, at the old Flamingo Hotel in Worcester, Massachusetts. I understand that the hotel burned down years later, but I do not know in what year.

I was told that my birth mother was Mary Saucier, an Italian woman who was married to Harold Saucier, a Polish man. My mother had an affair with a black man, and she became pregnant with me. I can't even imagine what my mother's husband thought or how he felt about her affair and pregnancy.

Back in the fifties, interracial marriages, let alone illicit affairs, were not acceptable. I don't know what the relationship between my biological parents really was, because no one ever discussed them with me. I don't know if they loved one another and had an ongoing relationship or if I was just the product of a one-night stand. I guess that it really does not matter what the circumstances were; the fact is that I was not wanted, and I was abandoned.

In later years, I learned that at the time of my conception and birth, my biological mother worked as a waitress and her husband was a painter in Worcester.

I am not sure why my mother was permitted to bring the pregnancy to term. I am assuming that she and her husband were not living together at the time, but nevertheless, I was born at the old Flamingo Hotel, so I was told.

Shortly after my birth my mother took me to a friend's house; she asked her friend to watch me for a while. She said that she had some errands to run and that she would be back soon, but she never returned to pick me up.

I was not immediately given the name or identity of my biological father. I have no animosity towards him because my parents who raised me told me that my biological father really loved me and wanted to take legal custody of me. But back in 1951, it was next to impossible for an unmarried black man to be granted custody of a child by the courts, especially an interracial child.

And in addition to that, my mother was married and her Polish husband would be deemed to be my legal father. Since my birth was not attended or recorded, I really didn't legally have a father or a mother.

I am not sure whether or not my biological mother's husband was aware that she was pregnant with a black man's child; no one ever mentioned that fact to me, ever.

My parents also stated that they had spoken with my biological father about taking me in and raising me, but they did not want him to be involved in my life or have any decision-making regarding me and my future.

They felt that it would be less confusing if he remained anonymous. Due to this and other reasons, my biological father agreed never to make any advances towards me in reference to his being my father, and he always respected my parents' wishes.

In later years, I was told who my biological father was, but I was never to refer to him as my father and I never discussed him with anyone.

I saw this man from time to time and he would always acknowledge me. He would ask me how things were going and how I was doing. I would always tell him, "OK," and he would say, "All right, be good, be cool, and stay out of trouble," and he would always give me ten to twenty dollars whenever he saw me. I never told my parents about his giving me money or the fact that I was communicating with him at all. I never deliberately sought him out, but I was always pleased to see him and get some money.

I always had a distant relationship with my biological father once I knew who he was, but neither one of us ever mentioned the fact that he was my father or not even that we were related.

Can you imagine being a young child, seeing your biological father, and not being able to embrace him or let him know how much I needed his love? I felt like a lost puppy, and I didn't know how to handle my feelings. I felt so much pain, especially when I saw my friends interacting with their fathers; the hurt was unimaginable. I just kept everything bottled up inside and tried to be a big guy.

My biological father was some sort of special police officer. He was part of the community and worked at the club downstairs from Ma Levesey's apartment, when they had parties.

My adoptive parents, Amorite and Nellie Johnston, were both born and raised in North Carolina.

My mother, Nellie Brooks (Gray) Johnston, was the daughter of Elijah and Emma Roberts Brooks. She was born on February 6, 1909, and was raised in Gastonia, Gaston County, North Carolina, near the Crowders Mountain State Park.

My mother, Nellie Brooks Gray Johnston
(Photo courtesy of Josie Brooks)

My father, Amorite Johnston, was born on June 13, 1913, and raised in Charlotte, North Carolina. I do not recall who his parents were but the family resided in Charlotte. My father was a big, strong, strapping man whom I looked up to, and I wanted to be just like him when I grew up.

After my adoptive parents married, they moved north to Worcester, in hopes of finding work and having a better life, but they were never able to have any children of their own.

Amorite Johnston: My adoptive father

My adoptive parents were already in their mid-forties when they took me in sometime in the year of 1953 or 1954. Since I had spent the first two and a half years of my life with other families, I am assuming that I went to live with the Johnston family in the winter of 1953 or early in 1954.

My first memories were not always good ones. I have had some very traumatic episodes in my life, and that is why I sometime questioned why I was here and what my purpose was.

After my mother abandoned me at her friend's house, I was given to the Grady (Johnson) family. My new family was headed by a single mother, Miss Ethel Mae Grady (Johnson). I stayed with the Grady (Johnson) family for about one year. Miss Grady (Johnson) had a son by the name of Harry Johnson, who became one of my best friends later in life.

After the first year of my life, I was given to the Richardson family, which was headed by Clarence and Helen (Wilson) Richardson. I stayed with the Richardson family for about one and a half years.

The Richardson's had two daughters and a son. The girls were named Ethel and Clarice, and the boy was named Charles "Buster" Richardson. Buster was six years old than me, and I always considered him to be my big brother, and we remained very close up until his death in May 2007.

After the first two and a half years of my life, I was taken in by the Johnston family. The Johnston family gave me the name of Robert Edward Johnston, but never legally changed my name or adopted me.

I never knew what I was called prior to being named Robert Edward Johnston around the age of two and a half to three years.

Me as a baby with the Richardson family
(Photo courtesy of Robert Johnston)

CHAPTER 1:
First Memories

One of my first memories was being in Harry's house, the Grady (Johnson) family. I think that I was spending the night with them. I must have been about three years old and I recall being in a very small room. I remember saying my prayers: "Now I lay me down to sleep, I pray the Lord my soul to keep."

I also recall Ma Levesey. Ma Levesey babysat four neighborhood children, which included me, one other boy, and two girls. Ma Levesey dipped snuff and listened to soap operas on the radio.

One day the boy, I don't recall his name, and I stole some of the snuff so that we could mimic Ma Levesey. Well, needless to say, that was not a good idea. We got so sick and our heads burned from the snuff, and in addition to that, Ma Levesey spanked and scolded us.

The next memory that I had was when I was riding on the back of a little boy's tricycle. We went down a small hill and when we came back up and stopped the tricycle, a bird defecated on my arm. Well, I thought that the world had come to an end, but everyone around me just laughed.

9

Ethel Johnston (left, 1976; right, 1994):
the first lady who kept me after I was abandoned

(Photos courtesy of Harry Johnson)

Harry Johnson: son of the first lady who kept me

My mother had always kept me very neat and clean, and I could not bear having the bird's waste on me. I jumped off of the back of the tricycle and ran home crying.

My mother heard me screaming and ran outside to see what was happening. I showed her the bird feces on my arm, and she immediately took me inside, cleaned me up, and changed my clothes.

Some of the children in the neighborhood had fifties motorcycle hats. Calvin, a kid I knew, had one and I wanted it. I snatched the hat off of his head and ran with it. I slipped and fell on a piece of slate and cut my right wrist; I still have that scar today. Calvin caught up with me when I fell and took his hat back.

Another thing that stood out vividly in my mind was that the ice and rag men would come around with horse-drawn wooden carts every day. The ice man would pick up large blocks of ice with a large iron tong and take it upstairs and place it in the refrigerator.

The rag man would collect old rags and pieces of cloth from people, which he would resell.

We always got excited to see the ice and rag men because we enjoyed talking to and playing with their horses.

The Johnston's lived in a six-family brick apartment building at #53 Clayton Street, Worcester, Massachusetts. They lived on the third floor on the right side.

Across the street from the Johnston's apartment building was the Masonic Lodge, where the area Nipmuc Indians would have pow wows' and other Indian affairs in their native dress. The Indians would dance outside on the streets sometimes, and we would all go downstairs to watch them.

One of our neighbors on Clayton Street was Miss Logan. Miss Logan lived on the first floor and also babysat me from time to time. Miss Logan had a black Belgian shepherd dog by the name of "King." King was feared by everyone in the neighborhood. King was very protective of the people he knew, and when King showed up at the Thomas Street School yard, everyone would leave.

There was also a small club downstairs under the apartments in the Johnston's building.

The next street up from Clayton Street was Laurel Street; they were cross streets. The entire neighborhood consisted of black families with the exception of two white families. There were a couple hundred blacks in the neighborhood at the time.

The atmosphere on Clayton and Laurel Streets was that of one big happy family unit. Everyone took care of each other. Each parent would look out for all of the children in the neighborhood. If we were doing something wrong or causing problems, the parent would correct us and then take us home to our parents, where we would get further punishment. I recall that it was a very happy time for everyone, especially the children.

Every weekend there was always a party going on somewhere. I recall that we had a water balloon fight at one of the block parties; the Clayton Street kids competed against the Laurel Street kids, and we had a blast. The neighborhood had block parties and activities all of the time, and it was a really happy period in all of our lives.

All of the neighborhood children knew each other, and we would all gather in the Thomas Street School yard in the afternoons and on weekends to play with one another.

I met three of my best friends at a block party held on the Thomas Street School yard. They were Luther A. D. Ward, III, Kenny Johnson, and a boy that we all called "Fatty."

Luther A. D. Ward, III and I met when we were about seven or eight years old. Luther was not a very poplar guy because he did not sing like some of the other guys, but I liked him as a person. Luther was a very smart kid; he had a brain and always worked to earn his own money. Fatty and I would tease and make fun of Luther because he worked as a cleanup boy at the Prospect House and would only get paid every two weeks. Fatty and I would call Luther "The Cowboy Guy;" we thought that it was so funny for him to work and only get paid every two weeks.

Luther's father was named Luther A. D. Ward, Jr. and was born in Grafton, Massachusetts, about eight miles from Worcester; his mother's name was Elizabeth Toney Ward. Luther had three sisters, JoAnne, Barbara, and Deadra, and two brothers, Michael and Jimmy. Luther's family lived on Newberry Street, but later moved to Laurel Street, where we met.

Luther's parents were divorced when he was very young, and he was not allowed to come out to play at night during the week because his mother had to work at night to support the family. Luther's sisters had to baby sit the younger children while their mother worked. Sometimes the guys and I would go over to Luther's house to visit when his mother was at work because he had sisters that we wanted to see.

We had a neighborhood dog that we named "Brownie" because he was brown. Brownie was the sweetest dog in the world. He was loved by everyone and the entire neighborhood fed and took care of him. He followed the children around everywhere they went and was very protective of them.

One day, for some unknown reason, someone threw lye on Brownie and he was badly burned. Luther's mother found out that Brownie was hurt and she took him to the hospital, where he had to have surgery. I don't know for sure who paid for the surgery; I think that maybe the entire neighborhood helped out because everyone loved Brownie so very much. I don't know what finally happened to Brownie; I lost track of him as I grew older and started hanging out on the streets with the older guys.

I was a very mischievous child and was always getting into trouble. Luther, Kenny, and I with a few other neighborhood kids decided to steal some grapes from a man who lived in the neighborhood. We sneaked into the neighbor's yard and started eating grapes from his vine. I don't recall the man's name, but he saw us and came out with a barber's leather strap and started chasing us. We were all frightened when we saw the leather strap, and we ran away as fast as we could. But the man caught up with Fatty and whipped him with the belt; we could hear Fatty screaming, but we never looked back. We were all around eight years old and were too afraid to go back to help Fatty, so we continued to run until we reached our homes.

At some point, I don't recall exactly when, Luther and his family moved to the projects in Great Brooke Valley, and we lost contact with each other in middle school.

Gramps Pool Hall was a very popular hangout on Laurel Street where people played pool and cards. I loved to play pool at Gramps and I was pretty good at it.

Further down Laurel Street was the Elk's Lodge and around the corner was Agnes's. Agnes's served food and liquor and also had parties. The people would eat upstairs and go downstairs to play the jukebox and party.

A shoe shop was also on Laurel Street. I don't recall its name, but I recall that it was there.

Mr. Sets owned a very small grocery store on Laurel Street. Some of my friends and I would go into Mr. Sets' store and steal candy and cookies when he was not looking.

On the corner of Laurel and Clayton Streets was a store called Uppetts. Uppetts sold bread, milk, candy, ice cream for 5 cents a cone, kerosene for the heater, and a lot of other supplies.

I also recall stealing candy from Uppetts, but thank God I never got caught.

I learned a lot at Buddy's Barber Shop. We had to sit still and be quiet in the shop and listen to the older men tell stories and talk about their lives. Most of the men living in our neighborhood came from down South, and they had a lot of stories to tell about how they grew up on the farm and how difficult it was being raised in the South.

They also talked about how prejudiced the white folks were in the South and how the white men would hang black men and have their women. I was too young to understand what they were talking about, but it sure didn't sound good.

My father's brother Floyd Johnston was a part-time barber in Buddy's Barber Shop. Sometimes I would go to the barber shop to visit my uncle and just sit around listening to all of the stories being told by the men getting haircuts or just hanging out.

Lucille's Beauty Salon was adjacent to the barber shop. My mother did not go to the beauty salon; she had a hot stove and curling irons at home and would fix her own hair.

The Johnston's were unable to have children of their own, but they took me in and they tried to give me love and everything material that they could afford.

My mother was a very kind and loving woman, but she was also very stern. She worked hard and took very good care of the home and family.

My mother worked most of her life as a domestic for an attorney and several other families in Worcester. The rest of her time was devoted to her family and the church.

My father worked as a janitor for Wyman Gordon, a manufacturing company that made parts for airplanes. His salary was sixty-five dollars a week at the time.

When I was around age thirteen, I recall my father showing me a $200 paycheck. He told me that it was more money than he had ever had at one time in his life. He explained to me that the union had come into Wyman Gordon and he had been promoted to another job and had been given a pay raise.

As a young boy I never really had any chores to do; I just played with my toys. From the beginning, I was spoiled rotten. My parents gave me everything I needed (including a whipping when I deserved it). I was usually allowed to have my way until I got completely out of control. My mother would then try to discipline me with a rough hand and physical spankings, which got more severe with my age.

I don't recall ever seeing my parents displaying physical love towards one another, and I never heard them say that they loved each other. I also did not receive physical or verbal displays of love towards me from my parents. I guess that it was assumed that we loved each other by just being together as a family.

Another thing that stuck out in my mind was the fact that I realized that my parents did not sleep in the same room. I don't know why this stuck out in my mind, except I noticed that my friend's parents were sleeping in the same bedroom. My father snored very loud; I mean he really snored loud, and I guess that was the reason why they were not in the same room.

We were the first family in our building to have a television. On Friday nights my father's friends would come over to the apartment to watch the *Gillette Friday Night Fights* on TV. My father and his friends drank alcohol, but my mother would never allow it inside the house, so the men would have their drinks before coming over to watch the fights. They were usually lit up very well before they arrived at the apartment.

The best Christmas that I ever had in my entire life was when we lived on Clayton Street. I was around five and a half years old at the time. That year I took a picture with Santa Claus, and I got so many toys and things for Christmas; I couldn't even imagine a Christmas that good. I mean it was a huge Christmas; I mean huge.

My first picture taken with Santa Claus
(Photo courtesy of Robert Johnston)

'Cowboy Bobbie' Christmas 1957
(Photo courtesy of Robert Johnston)

I received a black bike with training wheels, a wagon, boxing gloves, toy soldiers, clothes, a cowboy outfit with guns, and lots of other gifts. I thought in my mind that my parents must have really come into some big money that year.

The family attended John Street Baptist Church, and my mother also held weekly prayer meetings on Thursday nights at our apartment.

While my mother was conducting her weekly prayer meetings I would sit in my room with my toy cars and listen to the service. I was not permitted to make any noise during the service and therefore, I could not really play with the cars because they would make too much noise on the wooden floors.

My mother was a strict disciplinarian, and she would not hesitate giving me spankings when I got out of line, so I had to be quiet.

As a young man I sang in the junior choir at John Street Baptist Church. The junior choir was very good, and we traveled around quite frequently on Sundays and weeknights to different area churches with the pastor to sing.

We traveled to Connecticut; Providence, Rhode Island; Boston; Springfield, Massachusetts; and other churches in the general area around Worcester.

Some time between my sixth and seventh birthday, my mother and some of the ladies at John Street Baptist Church had a disagreement over something at the church. I think that it was about money, but I am not really sure.

As a result of that dispute, my mother and some other ladies left John Street Baptist Church and established another church. Their church was called Second Baptist Church and is still in operation today.

Even though I wanted for nothing, there was always an emptiness and yearning in my heart to belong. I had no brothers or sisters, and I was usually alone or with an adult person. I always longed for a family of my own, a family which no one could ever take away from me.

I recall as a young child that my parents would take me to North Carolina every summer on vacation to visit their relatives. Their family was very large, and I had a lot of cousins to play with in the country. We would stay in North Carolina for one or two weeks every year.

Even before I was taken in by my parents, they were spending their summer vacations in North Carolina. The trips were very long, but they were very exciting.

I would sit in the back seat of our car and look out the window at the beautiful scenery on the way to North Carolina. I have always enjoyed nature.

The sight of fog lifting over the mountains in the early morning was amazing. I felt like I was the most important person in the world.

I would ask my parents for a soda pop and we would stop along the way to get my soda. I always saw my father enter through the back door of stores; I didn't know why. I didn't understand racism at the time, but I later learned how evil and destructive it can be.

Upon arrival in North Carolina, we were always greeted like a royal family by the relatives. I had tons of cousins with whom I could play. The family would have cookouts, and we would all eat outside under the large oak trees. The children would run around in the yard and play in the woods all day, and we would sometimes go to Erwin Park in Gastonia to have a cookout and swim.

On Sunday morning, our parents would take us all to the Ebenezer Baptist Church in Kings Mountain, North Carolina, where some of the families were members. I didn't like going to church, but I really enjoyed my summers in the country.

My mother had two sisters, Maude Brooks Spikes Gordon and Flossie Brooks Stewart, and six brothers, Will, Roy, Leonard, Wayne, Roosevelt, and Paul Henry Brooks.

Uncle Paul and his sisters Maude and Flossie lived across the road from each other on the family's land near Crowders Mountain State Park.

Aunt Maude Brooks Spikes Gordon
(Photo courtesy of Josie Brooks)

Aunt Maude Brooks Spikes Gordon had four daughters, Florence Adams, Olivia Moultrie, Ruth Byrd, and Grace Stanley.

Aunt Maude had eight grandchildren and eighteen great-grandchildren at the time of her death in November 1988.

Aunt Flossie Brooks Stewart had two sons, Lawrence and John Brooks.

I didn't spend a lot of time playing with Lawrence and

John because they were much older than me.

Aunt Flossie had thirteen grandchildren and seventeen great-grandchildren at the time of her death in March 1988.

Uncle Will Brooks was married to Josephine Lathan. They had two daughters, Louise Brooks (Friday) and Edna Brooks (Brown), and six sons, Lewis, Howard, Beauford, Oliver, Ecnera, and Fred Brooks.

Aunt Flossie Brooks Stewart
(Photo courtesy of Josie Brooks)

Uncle Roy Brooks and his wife had two daughters, Ruth and Inez Brooks.

Aunt Josephine Lathan Brooks
(Uncle Will Brooks' wife).
(Photo courtesy of Josie Brooks)

Paul Henry Brooks married a lady by the name of Carrie Janie Moore.

Aunt Janie and Uncle Paul Brooks met at the Gethsemane Baptist Church in Gastonia, when she was eighteen years old and Uncle Paul was thirty years old. They dated for a year and a half and finally got married in 1937. After getting married, Aunt Janie and Uncle Paul moved into the house with Uncle Paul's mother, Emma Roberts Brooks, in the Crowders Mountain State Park area of Kings Mountain. They then had a total of eleven children: four boys (Clyde Roger, Carl Lee, Luther Evon, and Wayne Walter) and seven girls (Carnel, Prince, Janette, Lillian, Doris, Paulette, and Vernice).

At the time of Uncle Paul's death in March 1993, they had a total of twenty-two grandchildren and ten great-grandchildren.

I especially enjoyed my mother's sister-in-law, Aunt Carrie Janie Moore Brooks. "Aunt Janie," the name, by which she is still called by everyone, has always been dear to my heart. Aunt Janie was such a kind-hearted and loving woman. She was a mother to everyone who knew her. Her spirit was always very uplifting in every way. Aunt Janie always showed me lots of love, even though I was a very mischievous child.

My mother and I would stay at Uncle Paul and Aunt Janie's house while my father visited with his mother and family in Charlotte.

Drawing of the country of Aunt Janie and
Uncle Paul Brooks in the 1950s
(Drawing courtesy of Aunt Janie Brooks)

Uncle Paul was a farmer and Aunt Janie was a homemaker, and she also helped out on the farm. They lived on about twenty-eight acres of land, where they raised cotton and vegetables. Uncle Paul also rented out other land and share-cropped with Mr. Yumon Lind to help make ends meet. They would also go door-to-door selling their vegetables and wild berries that they had picked. A gallon bucket of blueberries would sell for about a $1.00, and a gallon bucket of blackberries would sell for $0.25.

Aunt Janie and Uncle Paul Brooks
(Photo courtesy of Aunt Janie Brooks)

My two favorite cousins were Wayne and Janette Brooks, because we were very close in age. Cousin Wayne and I were very close, and I always enjoyed playing with him.

One day Wayne and I made bows and arrows out of some sticks and decided to shoot the bees that were flying around the eaves of Aunt Janie's house. Well, I looked down and saw a bee on my sneaker and before I could move, the bee crawled up my pant leg. At that point I

Cousin Wayne Brooks
(Photo courtesy of Carl Brooks)

Me and Cousin Janette Brooks
(Photo courtesy of Robert Johnston)

had a royal fit; I undressed myself right there in front of everyone. I was hollering and screaming like a mad person, and everyone came running out of the house to see what was happening. My mother and my Aunt Janie picked me up and took me inside of the house. They finally got me calmed down and put my clothes back on.

Some of my other cousins would come from Dallas and Charlotte, and we would run and play outside most of the day. I recall playing with Robert and Edward, Uncle Lawrence's sons from Charlotte, and my Cousin Josie, Uncle Lewis Brooks' only daughter. Uncle Lewis was the son of Will Brooks, Uncle Paul's brother, and he was married to Josephine Latham Brooks. Uncle Lewis and his family lived in Dallas.

Robert, Edward, Josie, and some of Aunt Janie's girls would beat my tail because I was such a spoiled brat. I would run away from them and look for a weapon to defend myself. I would find a big stick and return to the battlefield to fight. I would try to hit my cousins with the stick, and they would run away pretending to be afraid of me. I thought that it was so funny; I had the big guys on the run. Of course, they were pretending; they just wanted to make me laugh.

All of the children stayed together when we played outside because there were lots of copperheads and rattlesnakes in the Crowders Mountain area. The older children were responsible for taking care of the younger children.

Cousin Josie would help to take care of me because I was very young and was from the city; I did not realize the dangers of country living.

Uncle Paul and Aunt Janie had lots of fruit trees around the house, and we would constantly pick and eat fresh fruit from the trees. We also had lemonade and lots of cookies to eat throughout the day.

I also had a big crush on my cousin Carnel, who was about fifteen years old. Cousin Carnel was tall and she was the most beautiful girl that I had ever seen. I really loved Carnel, and I thought that she belonged to me, and I always wanted to be near her. When Carnel would go out at night I would refuse to go to bed until she returned home. I would tell my mother that I couldn't go to bed until Carnel came home because I had to see her and make sure that she was okay. Once she arrived home and I was able to say goodnight to her, I was able to go to bed and sleep well. My mother and Aunt Janie were tickled to death that I had such a crush on Carnel.

Aunt Janie and Uncle Paul always sacrificed everything to raise their children and did not have any extra money to spend on themselves. When Aunt Janie and Uncle Paul celebrated their fiftieth wedding anniversary, their daughter Prince made a beautiful, beautiful gown for Aunt Janie to wear.

For the first time in Aunt Janie's life, she bought something that she really wanted. She had seen a pair of shoes that she wanted, and she said to herself, "Now look-a-here, do you know one thing, the Lord has blessed you to get this far and all the kids are grown and now it's your time." From that day forward, Aunt Janie bought what she wanted and didn't ask anyone for permission.

Her children knew how much she had sacrificed to raise them and get them educated, and they appreciated what she had done. They knew that Aunt Janie had gone without, and when they grew up they would always buy lots of beautiful clothing and other beautiful things for her.

Cousin Inez Brooks, Uncle Roy's daughter, married a Mr. Cornelius, who everyone called 'Tonk,' and they moved to New Jersey. Inez and her husband worked very hard and sacrificed a lot to save their money. They would actually go without things that they needed just to save money, and they eventually became very wealthy. They later relocated to Baltimore. Inez and her husband did not have any children, and it was assumed that when they passed away, her sister Ruth inherited their estate.

Cousin Lawrence went into the military and when he returned home, he got married to a lady by the name of Martha and they moved to Charlotte. Cousin Lawrence was a self-employed contractor and worked as a concrete finisher. He and his wife raised their eleven children in a two-bedroom house in Charlotte.

All together, the Brooks family totaled more than one thousand members in the Cleveland, Gaston, and Mecklenburg county areas.

At the end of our summer vacation I was always a little sad to leave my cousins, especially Cousin Wayne, but I quickly changed my mind once we were on our way back to Worcester. I enjoyed playing with my cousins, but I liked being at home with my friends even better.

I always knew that I was different as a child, but I didn't understand the difference until I actually started attending public school.

In September 1956 at the age of five, I was enrolled in kindergarten in the Worcester Public Schools and my teacher was a Mrs. Sadye Fielding.

From the beginning of the year, I was a disciplinary problem. My attention span was very poor because I was not interested in school. I had the ability to do good work, but I would not apply myself; I wanted to stay at home and play.

I was always excellent with the spoken language and enjoyed music and science. But I had difficulty with regards to being obedient, working well by myself and with others, fair play, respect for others and regulations, and respect for the rights and property of others. After all, I had always had my way at home and with my parents, usually, and I felt that I had the same rights at school; I didn't understand the difference.

In the summer of 1957, after returning from our annual trip to North Carolina, my parents decided to move to the west side of town. My mother thought it would be better because supposedly the better black folk lived there.

The family moved from the east side to an apartment on the west side, our new address was #22 Bancroft Street, Worcester.

Ironically, after moving to the west side, the kids started stealing my toys. But on the east side, which was considered to be the bad neighborhood, I never had a toy stolen.

The Davenport family from North Wilkesboro, North Carolina, lived on the third floor. Their son Walter and I became friends.

The Schuyler family lived on the second floor, but they moved after about a year.

The Gunn family from Reidsville, North Carolina, moved to the second floor. Mr. Gunn had a large pot belly. He could smoke a cigarette and hold onto the ashes until the cigarette was almost finished. It was amazing to watch.

Performing with my dance school
(Photo courtesy of Robert Johnston)

Mr. Gunn had two daughters, Roberta and Annie. His daughter Roberta was taking acrobat and tap dance lessons. Roberta was one year older than me, and Annie was one year younger than me.

Roberta Gunn and I became very good friends, and when I was in the fourth grade I started taking acrobatic and tap dance lessons with her. George and Tointon Hickey were my dance teachers. I enjoyed dance, but I didn't like being the only boy in the class.

While taking dance with Roberta, a Jewish man by the name of Murray Broder came to the school and took some of us to nursing homes and other places to perform and put on shows.

Mr. Broder was the owner of a candy distributing company in Worcester and he was involved in numerous community activities.

At the age of six, I joined the Ionic Avenue Boys Club, where I received a lot of good mentoring and learned how to swim. The annual fee of the Ionic Avenue Boys Club was two dollars ($2.00). I remained a member of the club until the age of fifteen.

I started attending the first grade at Winslow Sever Elementary School in the fall of 1957. Winslow Sever Elementary School was kindergarten through sixth grades. It was very apparent from the start that the teachers at Winslow Sever did not care what the color of your skin was; you were going to learn.

I received a rattan frequently. A rattan was a hit in the hand for being bad, being disruptive, or fighting. I would then go home and be punished again by my mother. During that time the teachers stayed in close contact with the parents, and they would constantly report my bad behavior to my parents; it was almost on a daily basis.

At the time I did not know why I was always fighting and causing trouble, but I guess that I just wanted attention.

Every Friday City Bank would come to Winslow Sever to teach the students how to make out bank deposits and save money. One Friday my mother would not give me any money because of something bad I had done, so I decided to steal the money. I was determined I would not be the only child in the class who did not have money to deposit into their bank account.

I went into my mother's room and stole a jar of pennies out of her cedar chest. Well, the pennies turned out to be a collection of Indian-head pennies in perfect mint condition. I could not get the pennies back and I ruined my mother's collection. My mother gave me a terrible whipping for stealing the coins.

I progressed as well as could be expected for a child who was not interested in school and who always had his head in the sky.

I always dreamed and thought about nature. I was fascinated by the wonders that I saw on the earth.

On July 16, 1959, at the age of eight years, I was baptized at Second Baptist Church of Worcester by Rev. Thurman A. Hargrove.

My parents were always involved in church and taught me the word of God, but I was not dedicated as my parents because religion and salvation did not mean very much to me at the time. However, my attitude towards religion and salvation would change in the later years of my life.

When I was around eight or nine years old, a friend and I decided to make some money selling non existent Christmas Stamps. We went around the neighborhood, took orders, and collected money for the nonexistent stamps. We had lots of money in our pockets and would always go to the store and buy ourselves some candy, cookies, and sodas.

We finally got caught when the pastor of Second Baptist Church called my mother to question her as to where the stamps were and when they would be arriving. It was getting close to Christmas and he wanted to mail out his cards.

As my mother hung up the telephone, she came to the back porch where my friend and I were sitting. We were eating the candy and cookies and drinking the sodas that we had purchased with some of the money we had collected. When cornered by my mother, we had to tell the truth; we couldn't lie because we were caught red-handed with the conned money and goods. My mother took my friend home and came back and got busy on my butt.

My parents had to take their money and repay the money that my friend and I had stolen.

It appeared that no matter what my parents did to help me, I just kept getting worse. There was a force driving me that I had no control over.

CHAPTER 2:
RACISM

In the summer of 1960, as usual, my parents took me to North Carolina with them for our annual vacation.

By this time I was old enough to understand racism and the negative effect that it can have on a child. I was what appeared to be a white child with black parents, and I would get constant stares and hear negative remarks directed towards me and my parents. The constant racial slurs being directed towards me, coupled with my low self-esteem and physical abuse, was driving me deeper into a path of self-destruction.

I recall an incident which took place during the trip which was very frightening and racist. I think that I was about ten years old at the time of this incident.

We had an old 1956 or 1957 Ford that had no air conditioning. It was extremely hot, and my mother's feet were swollen and she had a severe headache from the sun.

We pulled over next to a pharmacy in a town somewhere in Virginia. My mother instructed me to go into the pharmacy and get a small compact box of Anacin, which were sold in tiny tin boxes measuring about an inch to an inch and a half. The boxes contained about nine to ten Anacin.

I proceeded into the store and asked the man behind the counter for the Anacin, but his reply was, "We don't serve Niggers." My reply to him was, "Fine, but I do not want Niggers; I want Anacin's." The man continued to explain to me that they don't serve Niggers, and this exchange went back and forth between us a few times, and at that point I started to lose my temper; I was getting an attitude. I could see that at the same time, the man was getting nervous.

There was an opening around on the side of the counter, and while the man continued to tell me that they did not serve Niggers, he discretely handed me the tin box of Anacin around the counter. I understood and took the Anacin and left the store.

Evidently someone in the store had noticed the man giving me the box of Anacin because when I got outside I heard a commotion from inside the store. There was loud screaming and arguing between some men inside the store about the man giving me the box of Anacin. The man who helped me was fired and physically thrown out of the store and was told, "Since you want to serve Niggers, then go be with them." I turned and looked at the man, but at that point, I really didn't know what to say. I just sort of shrugged my shoulders at him and proceeded to get back into the car.

On that same trip to North Carolina, another incident occurred that stayed in my memory. It was raining so hard that we could barely see the road in front of us. The rain was coming down in buckets and my father had to pull off of the road to avoid having an accident.

My father noticed a restaurant and we stopped and went in to get out of the weather. As soon as we got inside we were stopped, and again as before, we were told that they did not serve Niggers. I immediately started to protest. My mother quickly put her hand over my mouth, grabbed me, and took me outside. I heard the man in the restaurant say to my father to drive for about another mile down the road and there would be a place that was owned by Niggers, who would serve us. We got back into the car and proceeded slowly down the road to the black-owned restaurant, where we stopped to eat and wait out the storm.

We finally arrived safely in North Carolina and were greeted warmly by the aunts, uncles, and cousins.

One afternoon my cousins and I were taken to the Joy Theatre in downtown Kings Mountain. This was the only theatre in the Town of Kings Mountain, and it was segregated.

1950s view of downtown Kings Mountain
(Photo courtesy of The Mountaineer Partnership)

Joy Theatre
(Photo courtesy of The Mountaineer Partnership)

There were separate entrances for the whites and blacks; One door had "Whites only" written over it, and the other door had "Coloreds only" written over it. I also noticed that the coloreds had to pay more than the whites to see the same movie.

Once inside the theatre, the blacks were also required to pay more than the whites at the concession stand for the same candy, popcorn, and drinks.

The theatre was sectioned off with plywood; the whites were seated downstairs and the blacks were seated upstairs in a dark balcony. The coloreds section was filthy and appeared to have never been cleaned. I got up to look over the partition into the whites section, and my cousins were all trying to stop me and told me not to do that, because I would get into trouble and get thrown out of the theatre. I was curious to know what was in the white section.

I looked over the partition and saw that the whites section was clean and well maintained. I really got angry about the difference and wanted to know why the coloreds had to pay more to sit in filth. I already knew the answer and I didn't like it.

If you dropped a kernel of popcorn on the floor in the coloreds section, the rats would come out like it was a football game. They would all be trying to get the kernel of popcorn.

Back in Worcester I played Little League baseball. I had one white coach, Mr. Fields, and two black coaches, Mr. Schuyler and Mr. Wright. Mr. Schuyler and Mr. Wright drafted me and most of the black players to their team. I played on the team for two years and I was pretty good. I played two positions: pitcher (left handed) and first baseman.

We had gotten good enough to play for the championship, but I could not participate because I was out of town with my parents in North Carolina for our annual vacation. I was very upset when our team lost the championship by a narrow margin, because I felt that we would have won if I had been there to help.

We arrived back in Worcester and I immediately went to see my team mates to talk about the championship game. I wanted every detail as to what had taken place. I really felt bad that we had lost the game, but we were planning to win the next year.

By the time I started the sixth grade at age eleven, the principal already had a notebook of complaints on me. I was constantly fighting and causing trouble in school.

On one occasion I got into an altercation with one of my class-mates. I don't recall what the fight was about, but it happened at recess. It was probably over some game that we were playing. I was trying to cut him with my banana knife when the principal got in between us to stop the fight. Instead of cutting my class-mate, I nicked the principal and cut his shirt. I was expelled for that day.

My parents were contacted and asked to come to the school to discuss the matter.

The principal stated that he did not want to press charges against me, but he wanted my parents to handle it and stop me from fighting.

Again my mother tried to beat the devil out of me, but it did not help. I was determined that I was going to fight no matter what happened. The beatings by my mother just made me angrier.

I started attending Chandler Street Junior High School in the fall of 1963 in an affluent Jewish neighborhood. I was involved in many, many fights while was at Chandler Street Junior High. I was attending school with lots of guys that I knew who were tough, and I wanted to maintain their friendship. Some of these guys were much older than me and I responded in the same way. If anyone looked cockeyed or smiled at me the wrong way, we were fighting whether they wanted to or not. I would fight just to prove what I thought at that time was my manhood and to impress the older guys.

I got into so many fights; for which there was no reason except that I wanted to fight. I was always looking for an excuse or a rea-son to fight, so if anyone even looked like they wanted to give me a reason or an excuse, I would jump on them. I not only jumped on the students, I also jumped on the teachers.

I did get expelled from school once for fighting and this was min-imal, since I fought all the time.

I recall one day at the start of the school year, I was fighting a boy in front of the school. I had straddled the boy, pinning him down with my knees on his arms; I picked up a brick and slapped him in the face with it, and he looked up at me and said, "You cheat." At that point I let go of him and got out of there, because by his response, I realized that there had to be something wrong in the cookie jar.

That same day, a few of my friends and I skipped school and went to find something to drink. We spent the day at one of my friend's house, drinking alcohol, smoking cigarettes and pot, and listening to music.

One day I went to visit my cousin Kenny Johnson, who had moved to Great Brooke Valley, and I ran into my friend Luther Ward. I was very happy to see Luther again, and we immediately reconnected. Luther and Kenny would come to hear me sing on weekends and we attended lots of house parties together.

Luther and I grew very close, and he was one of my closest confidants; we shared almost everything and I loved him like a brother. Luther and I remained close until he enlisted in the Marines in 1969. Luther had originally wanted to enlist in the Navy when he was seventeen years old, but his mother would not sign the necessary paperwork giving him permission.

As I grew older, I began to experience more and more the devastation of racism. Because I was biracial, living in a small segregated town, I was constantly being called derogatory names by both blacks and whites. The whites were especially cruel. Even my schoolteachers would ridicule me in front of my classmates. I gradually became a very angry and frustrated young man. I took my frustrations out on whomever I could. I was constantly getting into trouble, and my mother was at her wits end, attempting to disciple me and control my behavior.

The physical abuse by my mother got even worse. Sometimes she would beat me so badly that my father, who was a very silent man and who never interfered with her, would finally speak up and say, "Nellie, stop beating the boy, that's enough!"

Then the sexual abuse by my mother's friends started taking place. The first woman who sexually abused me was a friend of my mother's who was taking care of me while my mother was in the hospital having female surgery.

My father was in Charlotte with his mother, who was also very ill at the time, and I had to stay with my mother's friend.

On Halloween night in 1963 at the age of twelve, two of my friends and I broke into a neighborhood liquor store and stole a case of wine and liquor. We brought the wine and liquor back to the teenage club, which was on the corner directly across the street from my house. This club was a teen club run by Second Baptist Church. They served hot dogs, hamburgers, potato chips, and soda. There was a record player that we used to play records for the kids to dance.

I was allowed to attend the club when my parents were at home, so my caretaker permitted me to go to the club that night. This was the first night that the club opened at its new location. The club was previously located in the basement of the church. The new location was in a storefront underneath a three-family apartment building, which was owned by one of the members of the church, who rented the club out to the church for the teens.

We brought the wine and liquor back to the teen club and shared all but one gallon of the liquor with the rest of our friends. My two buddies and I drank the gallon of liquor, and I got loaded. When the teen club closed, I went to the house of the family that was taking care of me. When I arrived at the house, the husband was not there and the children were in bed asleep.

The woman directed me where to go to sleep and I did. The next thing I knew is that I was awakened by this woman being on top of me, kissing all over me, grabbing me and pulling my pants off, and she proceeded to have sex with me. I was approached several other times by that same individual after the first encounter and, because I was afraid and didn't want to cause any trouble, I just went along with it. The sexual encounters stopped when she realized that she and my mother were too close and she was concerned that it was too risky to continue.

The second incident was also at the age of twelve in the spring of the next year, about six months after the first incident. This encounter happened with the mother of one of my best friends. I went by to visit with my friend and his mother, but my friend was not at home and his mother was alone. She was not feeling well and asked me to run an errand for her. I went to the store and picked up what she had asked for. When I returned, we spoke generally for a few minutes, and she then told me that when she got better, she had two presents for me. She stated that she would tell me when to come by to get them, and I was not to tell anyone, because her children would get upset, because she never gave them gifts when they ran errands for her. Believing that she did not want to cause trouble between me and the kids, I agreed not to tell about the gifts.

A few weeks passed and one day while I was at my friend's house visiting, his mother told me when to come back to receive my two gifts.

At the appointed time I returned to the home of my friend. No one was at home except the mom. We talked generally again for about ten minutes, but I didn't recall the topic of conversation. I was then directed to go to the back hall, where I would find my gifts.

She had on a nightgown kind of robe, which was very common; there was nothing wrong or provocative about it. I went down the back hall as instructed and she followed behind me. She then proceeded to turn off the lights and told me to close my eyes and put my hands out. She said, "Put out your hands so that I can give you your gifts. There's nothing to be nervous about, don't be afraid." She then proceeded to take my hands and placed them on her breasts. She held my hands and started moving them across and around her breasts, she then kissed me.

I was frightened and I could see my being put back in the same situation as I had been before with the other woman, but I didn't know how to handle it.

I knew that I would not be able to say anything, because of the trouble that it would cause to my family and to her family, and because I had been in so much trouble before, I didn't know if anyone would believe me.

I was caught up in the same situation again, and I did not know what to do, so again I went along with what was happening. This woman also approached me several different times in the same manner. I wanted to stop going to her house, but I was afraid that if I stopped being friends with her son, that would draw too much attention and questions.

So I just continued the sexual activity with my friend's mother for about a year. The sexual encounters did not end until the family finally moved away.

I never told my parents or anyone else about the sexual abuse. I was too afraid of the trouble that it would cause, and I was just plain embarrassed for myself. There were other sexual issues that I was dealing with, and I just couldn't face what might happen.

To compensate for my feelings of loneliness and inadequacy, I got more and more involved with music. I began to sing in my room, and my mother would hear me and tell me to shut up, but I would keep on trying. When my mother realized that I was serious about singing, she started helping me and teaching me notes. I never studied music formally, but I gave it all that I had to give.

At the age of fourteen, I started hanging out heavily in my old neighborhood on the east side with the older guys, who let me join in with them singing. The west side was just too straight for me, and the guys were too square, and I didn't want to get into any trouble in my neighborhood.

All of the older guys who were getting into things were hanging on the east side so I would go there to hang out on the street corners with them. We would sing on the street in front of Uppetts on the corner of Clayton and Laurel Streets, at the Prospect House, and on the Thomas Street School grounds.

We would also build bonfires on the sandlot and sing at night. Luther, Kenny, Fatty, and the neighborhood kids would always come out to hear us sing. We were very popular, and we sang all types of songs by the Temptations, Smokey Robinson, the Supremes, and others.

In the middle of the school year, my parents moved to #34 Providence Street, which resulted in my having to change schools again. I left Chandler Street Junior High and started attending Grafton Junior High on Grafton Street in Worcester. I really didn't get into any fights at Grafton Junior High, and I think that it was because I was just beginning to really change and alter my focus more to music.

We lived next door to a Jewish synagogue. In the summertime I would have my window open to get some air, as it was hot and we had no air conditioning. The Jewish synagogue would also have their windows open, and they would start their services at 7:00 a.m. They would be playing their music and singing their songs, and I would get very upset with the noise. It took a while, but I finally got accustomed to the noise and realized that it was their church and that was the way they did things.

I enjoyed living on Providence Street because there were five apartment buildings, each with three floors filled with black people, which meant that there were fifteen black families living right together. There was also another building on the corner that housed another six black families. This was like having our own black neighborhood within a white neighborhood. It gave me a sense of pride to belong to the black neighborhood.

I was still hanging on the east side, which was probably a mile or two at the most from Providence Street. My visits to the east side got more and more frequent, since I was closer than when I lived on Bancroft Street.

I created new friendships and got involved with a new group of friends on the east side, who loved getting into trouble. The guys loved to steal, drink alcohol, and fight. That was just right down my alley. Anytime anyone white our age, or near our age, would come through the neighborhood in the evening or at night, we would jump on them and beat them up.

My parents knew that I was out at night, but they did not know what I was doing. They thought that I was just hanging out with my friends. My father had some questions about what I was doing because he would see me out sometimes with the older guys.

Since my father drank alcohol, but was not allowed to do so at home, I would sometimes meet him out drinking with his friends. He would be sitting on the corner directly across from the barber shop where there was a stone wall.

Behind the stone wall was a lot of dirt and sand and other things, and we called it a "Top Lot." But on the wall is where a lot of the older men would sit, talk, and drink their liquor. They weren't doing anything wrong, just hanging out and having fun.

My father had an idea that I was not being the nicest guy in the world and had even approached me a few times and told me, "Don't be doing anything that will get back to your mom that will hurt her. You know how your mother is. Be out, have fun, but be smart."

CHAPTER 3:
WHO AM I?

Something came up when I was around fourteen years old to make me ask about adoption papers; I don't really know what it was, but I started to question my parents about it and learned that I still had not been legally adopted.

I was given the name Robert Edward Johnston by my parents when they took me in, but I never had a birth certificate in that name.

My mother had signed for me to get a Social Security card and a driver's license because at that time no other proof was required to acquire the documents, just your parents' signatures.

At that point I began questioning my parents' love for me. I was totally crushed and felt that my parents didn't really love me either. Now I'm feeling that the white lady didn't want me because I wasn't good enough and got rid of me, and now they won't adopt me. This made me feel that I wasn't really good enough for them either.

I don't know how to explain it, but I just lost it. I totally started hating white people, and resentment towards my parents was growing, especially towards my mother.

Because of my pain, I really started fighting everyone for no reason at all. I mean I would physically, verbally, literally start fights just to fight. I guess I was deliberately trying to self-destruct. I hated myself and everyone around me. I started hanging out even more with the older guys on the street corners and tried to get involved in every negative situation that I could find.

At the same time, I was getting more involved with music and hung out with the older guys singing the old "Do Wops" in the back of trailers left in parking lots. We would get our wine and go up in the trailers, because they had a real nice "Tickle" in it, and do our do wops.

I had always had a passion for writing and I started to write poems to express some of my feelings. I was always looking for love and I longed for that one person who would love me unconditionally and who would never leave me alone.

I also had a very strong love and appreciation for nature. I loved New England in the fall; the scenery is mesmerizing. The changing color of the leaves, the briskness of the air, and the beauty of the surroundings warmed my heart. I was inspired and highly motivated to write on rainy fall days. When I sat in the window and watched the water beating against the window and hitting the trees, it moved me in a very special way.

I visited Cape Cod on a few occasions and also found a great appreciation for the water. I was able to sit on the beach for hours and just meditate and contemplate things happening in my life. I would be at total peace with myself and the world when I looked out over the vast ocean. I had never really been around a large volume of water until I was a grown man, and it was like being in heaven.

My self-esteem was very low, as I felt that no one truly loved me. I did not feel worthwhile, and I became withdrawn not only because I felt unloved, but I also felt inadequate.

I was also very shy and introverted. I had no sense of direction, literally. I could not find my way around easily and I could not follow written directions. I must be taken physically to the location and shown a few times before I am able to go on my own. I kept mostly to myself and had very few friends until I started hanging out on the streets.

You see, I had other issues that were major to me. I had been sexually abused by two of my mother's female friends. Both of these women were married and had children, and this made me feel worthless.

After leaving Grafton Junior High School, I attended Boyce Trade School, where I had to repeat the ninth grade, because you had to complete four years at Boyce Trade in order to graduate.

Boyce Trade School was an all-boys school. There may have been three girls in the school, who were studying printing.

I was hoping to get into the electrical or plumbing program, but for the first time in my life I had scored very high on the entrance exam. I would usually score between seventy-eight and eighty-two, but for some reason, I scored very high on the exam and I was placed in the drafting class, but I did not like it at all.

I stayed at Boyce Trade for a year and a half. While I was at Boyce Trade School, I got into several fights. Every challenge that potentially arose, I met it and dealt with it.

One challenge that arose was from a boy by the name of Russell. Russell was a white boy who had just recently been released from a reformatory school, where he had been sent for getting into an altercation with a police officer. When Russell arrived at school, he wanted to prove his manhood and figured that I was a good selection so he challenged to kick my butt. We fought and I broke Russell's jaw in several places, which required his jaw to be wired.

I was thrown out of school, expelled, and threatened with being arrested.

I told the school officials to do what they had to do, because we had a fair fight and I broke his jaw and I had witnesses that he threw the first punch.

The day afterwards, my parents took me back to school to meet with the principal. Russell was also there with his parents, and about twenty-five other students were there to confirm the exact same story that I had told. Russell had been the aggressor, not me, but Russell did not win the fight.

Based on the students' accounts of what had taken place between Russell and me, I was allowed to return to school with the promise that I would not get into any more fights.

It was again time for the family's annual vacation trip to North Carolina. We arrived without incident at my Aunt Janie and Uncle Paul's house.

Once in North Carolina, my cousins invited me out to a night-club. The name of the nightclub was "The Tijuana," and it was located on Highway 29/74 and Shady Grove Road. The Tiajuana nightclub had only one door and it served as both the entrance and exit doors. (Several years later the club's name was changed to the "Flamingo Club.")

I was dressed up pretty good in my pinstripe suit and a white straw brim hat. I was sitting at the table with two of my cousins when young ladies kept coming up to our table wanting to get introduced. I told them that I was not there for any trouble; I did not know them or who their boyfriends were, and I preferred not to get into any altercations that night because I didn't want to mess up my bad outfit.

It turned out to be a good decision not to get involved because about an hour later, a fight broke out at the club's doorway. Several people were shot and the fight advanced into the club. When I noticed that the doorway was relatively clear, I crawled, with my cousins behind me, out the door to keep from getting shot. We crawled all the way to our car; so much for saving my bad outfit.

While crawling across the club's parking lot, I noticed that there were two State Police cars sitting across the road on Highway 29/74 with what appeared to be nickel-plated shotguns. The officers sat there until the fighting subsided and they then left without entering the club. They did not come over to stop the fight, offer any assistance, or help the injured. It was my opinion, and that of others, that since it was a black assembly and no one white was getting hurt, they weren't getting involved and did not. The situation was extremely dangerous, but the officers totally ignored it and drove off.

While reflecting on the situation several years later, I thought, "How ironic; I was born at the Flamingo Hotel and I could have been killed at the Flamingo Club."

My last summer vacation trip to North Carolina with my parents was when I was about sixteen years old. I was no longer interested in going to North Carolina because I was involved with bands, hanging out on the streets with my friends, and had little jobs that I didn't want to quit.

On that last trip, I went to the supermarket with one of my female cousins.

My cousin and I were walking to the store when a young white man in the parking lot accelerated his vehicle and almost hit us. I felt that he had done this on purpose because I appeared to be a white man with a black female. I started to scream and curse at the man, and my cousin became very frightened. She said, "Shut up; you can't do that down here." I told her that I could do that anywhere I pleased to do it, and I was not going to let someone try to take me out and not have anything to say or do about it.

At that point, I was still in the mind-set of hating white people and was still looking for any reason to get into a confrontation with any of them. I felt that his actions were a justifiable reason for me to confront him, and I was ready, but my cousin finally convinced me to calm down. She kept telling me all the things that I could not do in North Carolina, and she was very scared for me and herself. I finally realized how frightened she was, and I then proceeded with her inside the store.

Once inside the store, I told my cousin that we should not go anywhere together again, because if anyone white bothered me or tried to hurt me again, I would not keep my mouth shut. If she did not feel safe with me, then we did not need to go out together again, as I would not back down from another fight.

On another day we went swimming at a "Coloreds-Only" pool in Kings Mountain. We were not allowed to go to the white swimming pool, which was much larger and in a better location. I really felt good about this, because I didn't like whites and did not want to be around them, because of how badly they had always treated me.

I found myself feeling good about a lot of things that were taking place in the South, especially the segregation. I didn't like the reason why it was taking place, but the results were to my liking.

Our summer vacation finally came to an end and it was time to return home. The car was loaded with our personal belongings and lots of fruits, vegetables, and canned goods given to us by Aunt Janie and Uncle Paul. The good-byes were long and heartfelt and we were finally on our way back to Massachusetts.

Following our established routine, my parents and I stopped in Baltimore to rest and visit with Cousin Inez and Tonk. I enjoyed seeing Cousin Inez and Tonk, but I was anxious to get back home to see my friends.

School would be starting soon and I wanted to have plenty of time to hang out on the streets with the guys. I was already making plans to get into some sort of mischief. I couldn't get into very much mischief in the country because I had too many people watching me and trying to keep me straight.

When we arrived back in Worcester I didn't wait to help unload the car. I immediately ran off to meet up with my friends.

On Labor Day in 1965 four of the older men and I, with three of the younger guys, went to the "Comic Strip" a teenage club in Worcester.

A group of white guys called "The New Breed" were singing at the club, and we asked if we could join in. To our surprise, the club owner said, "Yes," and we ad-libbed some Temptations songs, and we were a big hit.

After the show, the club owner asked if we would come back again for a special performance. We were very excited and were overjoyed at the opportunity. Three of us younger guys agreed to come back, but the fourth one was afraid.

Three of the older guys, Scottie, and I decided to form a group, and we called ourselves "The Young Temps."

The club owner arranged for us to perform at the Prospect House. He advertised the event in the newspaper and on the radio, and he even ordered tuxedos and shoes for us; we had the whole works.

When we arrived at the Prospect House to perform, we were sent downstairs to get dressed. Not only did we get dressed; we also got high on wine.

We eventually joined the first group and became known as "Bobbie, Scottie, and the New Breed." We sang at a lot of the clubs around Worcester; sang at high school functions, social functions, and weddings; and traveled throughout New England performing at different functions. I stayed with the group for about two years. I left when I became dissatisfied with the monetary payouts.

Scottie and I left the group and joined another band called "Herbies," with the agreement that we would all be paid equally. I sang with Herbies for about three years. While singing with

Herbies, Junior Graham, from Gastonia, joined the group. The band disbanded; because most of the guys were attending the Berkley School of Music and they were graduating and going on to pursue their careers in music. Some went on to play with Sammy Davis, Jr., Lou Rawls, and Joe Cocker. The organ player went on to become the conductor for the Vienna Philharmonic Orchestra.

Scottie, Junior, and I then joined an all-black band called "Soul Pepper." We were very disappointed with this band as their musicianship was not very good. We had been spoiled by the excellent musicians in the white bands. At that point I became disinterested in singing with the band and after about nine months I left the group.

Singing with the groups helped, but I still had a longing in my heart; something was still missing. I was becoming more and more angry with my parents and could not forgive them for not legally adopting me.

I was fifteen when I had my first fight with a black person. We were at a party being thrown for a girl who babysat for a young couple in the neighborhood. Even though the couple paid her for babysitting, they were also giving her a "Thank-You Party" at their house.

Some of the older guys in the neighborhood, about ten years older than me, also came to the party. One guy I had never seen before came to the party. I recognized that he was not a "Worcester Right"; he was a newcomer. People from Worcester were called "Worcester Rights," and this guy did not belong.

I was standing in the doorway and my arm was blocking his entry, and he asked me to move. I started to move when he said, "You better move or I will kick your f---ing ass." Noticing that he was much bigger and older than me caused me to be a little afraid, but I also noticed that my peers were there and this caused me to puff up. I said, "If you think you can do that, let's take it outside; I'm willing to take the ass whipping." I left and went downstairs with my friends, but the guy never showed up. I understood later that his friends did not permit him to come downstairs.

At that point, I was very angry, but I left with two of my friends to go to "O'Brien's", a diner in the neighborhood on Summer Street. O'Brien's diner was owned and operated by white people.

I went into O'Brien's and purchased a soda and some fries and proceeded to sit down to eat. As I sat eating, a few of the guys from the party came over and said, "Hey man, that guy from the party is over at Agnes's looking for you to kick your ass." I paid for my food and took off and ran to Agnes's. When I came into Agnes's, Agnes said, "Please go downstairs and shut that loud-mouth dude up. All he can say is how he wants to kick your butt. Please shut him up."

I went downstairs and started throwing punches at the dude, and he started ducking and tried to run. I grabbed him and threw him up against things—chairs, walls, whatever was there—and then I threw him up the stairs. I followed him and threw him outside into the street and told him, "Let's get it on now and get it over with now." Again, this guy is a lot older and bigger than me and I was really afraid, but my buddies were watching and I had to do what I had to do.

I started hitting him and this guy started acting like a baby. He starts covering up and almost crying; I mean, I'm beating on him and doing everything I knew to do, and he was cowering and covering up like a little baby. That really aggravated me that a grown man who threatened to beat my butt was now cowering and acting like a baby. I then knocked him down and kicked him; as I said, that was the first time that I had ever really fought with a black man.

I did not like fighting black people, but if you were white, let's get it on (if you were black, let's talk about it).

If you want to wrestle and tussle like that, fine, but I didn't like fighting black people. But this guy really provoked me, threatened me, and challenged me, and it made me angry when he turned out to be a coward.

By now I was fully involved in major criminal activity. I was just getting started with organized criminals. My friends and I would break into businesses and steal all that we could carry. We would steal cars and anything of value.

On St. Patrick's Day in 1967, my gang and I were on our way from one party to another. We heard music in the distance and decided to go see what was going on. We went into a club that was filled with white college students. We were told not so politely that we were not welcomed there and the bartender instructed us to leave.

We turned and started to walk out of the door when I was suddenly struck in the back with a bar stool.

There were twelve white boys and three black boys. The fight was on. We literally beat the stuffing out of those twelve white boys. The police were called, and we were all charged with disorderly conduct and turned over to our parents until our court date.

The twelve white guys were seventeen and older and were considered to be adults. They were tried in a different court from the three black boys, who were minors: sixteen and younger. The charges against the twelve white boys were dismissed, but when I came to trial, my attorney (the lawyer my mother worked for) recommended that I be given six months in reformatory school, stating that it might teach me a lesson.

When my father, who was normally a quiet and meek man, heard the attorney's recommendation, he stood up and protested loudly. He wanted to know from the judge why his son, who had been attacked, was being punished for defending himself and the boys who started the fight were let off. The judge ordered the records from the court proceedings for the twelve white boys and noted the physical condition of the boys. All twelve of the white boys were much larger, taller, and older than the black boys, but they had all sustained numerous physical injuries. They all had numerous bruises and one was even walking with crutches. The judge dismissed my case and advised us all to leave the courthouse and grounds separately, and if we did not we would be sent to reformatory school.

On another occasion, one Saturday night about ten white guys were coming through the neighborhood on Summer Street in Worcester. My buddies and I saw them, approached them, and started fighting with them for being in the neighborhood. My buddies left to go get some weaponry: sticks, pipes, bats, and whatever they could find to fight with.

A couple of the white guys took off and this left me there alone, confronting the other guys. Some of my buddies, realizing that I was there by myself, were on their way back when my biological father pulled up. He pulled up on the sidewalk in his car, and at that point not knowing that I was involved, he pulled out his gun and told everyone to stop and stand back. When he realized that I was in the middle of the fight, he called me over to his car and told the other boys to go home. He said, "Wherever you are from, go. Just get out of here and stop before I call the "Paddy Wagon" and have everybody arrested."

At that moment all of my buddies returned with their weapons and he sent them home.

My biological father then scolded me and told me how I could have been hurt badly or easily gotten killed. He asked me why we guys were bothering people and I told him that it was our hood and they got no business in our neighborhood. He then said to me, "They have a right to be anywhere they want to be, just like you have the right to be where you want to be." He gave me a very positive speech about what our attitudes were and explained that it was not our neighborhood, it was everybody's neighborhood, and we should not be fighting over something like that. He then told me to go home and he didn't want to ever see me fighting like that again.

I attended North High School in Worcester and graduated in June 1969. While attending high school I was constantly getting into trouble. I was involved in many, many fights, and my parents were always there to help me out when I got into trouble and got caught.

I had been abusing alcohol and smoking marijuana for several years when I started experimenting more and more with different types of drugs, like snorting cocaine.

I really didn't like snorting cocaine because I wanted something that would slow me down instead of making me more hyper. I tried speed, which I did not like for some reason, and I did not like the pill form of any drug.

I sniffed heroin a few times and liked it, but realized how addictive it was and decided not to use it on a regular basis. But from time to time, some friends and I would purchase a bag, split it up, and get high. We would put on some jazz music, nod, meditate, and groove with the music. A bag would keep us high for about two to three days, but I realized that I might become addicted and decided not to use heroin frequently. My drugs of choice were marijuana and heroin, because it would slow me down, relax me, and put me in a sedated state. I continued my use of illegal drugs for the next four or five years.

One night some of my friends and I stole a car to go for a joyride. After taking our ride we hide the car behind some trees and bushes and had planned to return the following evening to take another ride. When we arrived at the location where we had left the car it was no longer there. We didn't know if the police had found the car or if someone else had taken it.

We called the police and reported that a car fitting the vehicles description had tried to run us down. The Police Officer advised us that the car was stolen and that we should call them right away if we saw the car again.

We would steal from and take advantage of people just for the fun of it. To me it was just a big joke, as I had no respect for anything and did not care for anyone, not even myself.

I recall another incident when a group of about eight of us was walking up the street. We were approaching a hobby shop and when the store owner saw us coming he locked the door. The hobby shop owner called the police and the officer must have been right around the corner because he was there in a matter of minutes. We weren't even thinking about the hobby shop and we had no intentions of doing anything to the man or the shop.

The officer jumped out of his cruiser and left it running. The officer walked over to speak with us and we advised him that we were not trying to cause any problems; we were just walking up the street. While the officer had his back turned and was speaking with us one of the guys in the group got into the cruiser and crashed it into a wall. When the officer turned to run towards the cruiser, we all ran away.

Another time we broke into a business and stole all that we could carry by hand. In later years, I applied for a job with the same company and went to work for them.

My negative behavior and criminal activity escalated to a point where I got more and more involved in organized crime. At that point, I felt secure and protected by my fellow buddies. I was so angry by now that I did not care. I was set on a path of self destruction that lasted for what seemed like an eternity. I had no tolerance for anyone, and if I became angry enough, I didn't think that I would have hesitated to really hurt someone seriously.

I spent my graduation night from North High School sitting on Main Street on a curb stone. The reason that happened was because my principal approached me and told me that if I attended night school, along with my regular day school, and took English 4 and biology, I would have enough credits to graduate early at the end of my junior year.

I really would not have graduated early, but I would have graduated on time, since I had to repeat the ninth grade when I transferred to Boyce Trade School in the ninth grade. I would do anything to get out of school early, so I took the night classes.

It never occurred to me that I had a brain on my shoulders. I was taking a full load during the day and extra courses at night, and was passing with good grades. I was only focused on getting out of school.

After graduating from North High School, I had not made any definite plans to do anything. I just wanted to be out of school and free to roam. My friends were either going into college or the military; therefore, I decided that I needed to do something too.

I went down to the Selective Service Office to register for the draft, but later decided that I really didn't want to go into the military. I gave it a lot of thought and realized that the military would be too confining for me, and I really didn't want anyone telling me what to do. Now I needed to figure out a way to get out of going into the military.

I went to my mother's employer, the attorney, and told him what I had done and asked for his advice on how to get out of the draft. The attorney asked me, "Why did you sign up for the draft in the first place?" I told him, because I wanted to be like the other guys, but I didn't want to go to jail if I didn't report for duty.

The attorney said, "You aren't going to jail. How are they going to draft you?"

I said, "With the draft."

My attorney asked, "Whom are they going to draft?"

I said, "Me."

He asked, "Who are you?"

I said, "I am Robert Edward Johnston."

He said, "Prove it."

I said, "I can't because I don't have a birth certificate."

He said, "Exactly, and they can't either. They are not going to draft you plus you are an only child. You don't have to worry about anything bad happening with the military." He stated that if I should receive any paperwork from the military or get drafted, then I should come to see him.

This was during the Vietnam War era. At that time the military had a lottery draft system, where they would draw numbers out of a little round barrel. This was done on television and the slips contained birth dates. When they drew my birth date, it went into the 311th slot.

Shortly after the lottery, something was declared to be illegal and the drawing had to be redone. On the next lottery drawing, I was placed in the 400s and was never in a position to be called.

I never volunteered to go into the military, because my mother stated that she would do everything in her power to keep me out of the war, because I was her only child. Even though I was never legally adopted, I was all that my parents had, and they did love me very much, and my mother was not going to take a chance on losing me.

I knew that the military was just not my lifestyle and even though I never served, I have a great deal of respect and a deeper understanding for those who put their lives on the line to protect, secure, and make our country safe to live in.

At the same time, I was still involved in singing in bands and we performed at the "Kitty Cat Lounge," which was located on Main Street in Worcester and was the only black-owned club (other than the Elks Club).

There was a sense of pride when playing for black folk. The first time we played at the club, we let the white guys in the band start the night off by doing the first set without Scottie, Junior, and me.

When the blacks found out that the white guys were performing first, they didn't like it. The blacks would complain; they wanted to know why those white guys were going to perform first. They would say things like, "What are those white boys going to be doing up there? Man, they can't sing. We are going to laugh those white boys right out of here."

We knew how good those white guys were and just asked the black guys to just listen and give them a chance. When the band began to play, the audience went wild, because they recognized their superior musicianship and loved them. As a matter of fact, some of the guys in the band formed very good relationships with some of the blacks.

Having nothing really to do after graduating from high school, I decided to go to college. I didn't have any set goals in mind and really wasn't thinking about getting a better education; it was just something to do.

I enrolled in Worcester State University in 1970. At the time there were only three blacks attending the university. There was one other black boy, who was very quiet, and a black girl who just kept to herself. My English teacher was a white woman who did not particularly care for me, as I was very outgoing and blacks weren't really wanted at the school.

The first class was English, and I was about ten minutes late one morning due to having a flat tire on my way to the school. When I walked into the classroom, the teacher immediately stated that there was no way possible for me to pass her class, because my coming in late showed a lack of respect and concern for her and the class.

It was obvious that I had had some sort of problem; my clothing was dirty from changing the tire and everyone knew that I was always wearing clean clothes and kept up my appearance.

The teacher would not listen to anything that I had to say or excuse me from being late. In my mind I thought, "I don't have to be here and I'm certainly not going to take any crap from this prejudiced white woman." I just turned around and walked out of the classroom and the school; I never looked back.

After leaving Worcester State, I remembered that some people from the University of Massachusetts had come to my high school and gave us information on how to gain entrance into the university and explained how to get scholarships through the CEDA program. I did not know what the acronym stood for, but I went ahead and applied for the grant and was accepted; I was given minimal financial assistance based on my parents' combined income.

The University of Massachusetts was located in a beautiful setting out in the western part of the state. It was cold up there, but I really enjoyed the setting.

I enrolled at the University of Massachusetts at Amherst in the study of psychology.

I attended the university at the same time that Julius Erving, "Dr. J." attended. As a matter of fact, we were in the same dormitory, which was the John F. Kennedy Dorm.

I was in room 1809 and Dr. J. was in room 1909. Dr. J. was a very pleasant person who would stop and talk with you at anytime and never acted superior or as a superstar with any of his fellow students. He would also act as a referee at some of the intramural games.

I recall once in my freshman year, my friend Stevie Jenkins and I were standing looking out of the dorm window when we saw Julius Erving pushing a 1962 or '63 light blue Chevrolet towards the parking lot; it had obviously broken down and stopped running. Stevie and I went running downstairs to assist him, but we were too far away to get there in time to help him push the car. By the time we arrived downstairs, Julius had already pushed the car into the parking lot.

After Julius had his meeting with the Virginia Squires, we noticed that he was now driving a new light blue Cadillac. We learned later that he had signed with the American Basketball Association (ABA). I also recall that the ABA had the old multicolor basketballs at that time.

I was enrolled and attended the university, but I did not apply myself to my studies at all. I was still in a partying mood and did not care about anything.

After being accepted at U Mass, I was required to take a three-day orientation. During orientation I met a young man by the name of Sam who became my friend. Sam and I studied martial arts together at the university.

As a matter of fact, my friend Sam and I collectively came up with a scheme to get some free money. We knew that there was a lot of pot smoking going on by the students at the school and that a lot of the students were very naïve.

My friend and I came up with a plan to take a pencil and pad and go around to the dorm rooms pretending to be floor monitors. We would tell the students that we smelled marijuana and we were required to report them to the administration office.

The students would be so afraid that their parents would kill them if they found out about the pot smoking. Some of the students would cry and beg us not to tell on them. We would respond, "Hey what do you want us to do, lose our jobs and get kicked out of school?" We would threaten to have them expelled, take their marijuana, and coerce them into giving us money, watches, or whatever they had. We would sometimes make $1,500 in a week and would take the money and just have a party for ourselves.

I was still playing in bands, so I would leave the school on weekends and return on Monday. This limited my ability to get more money from the students.

At the school I also took black history, which was taught by a Jewish teacher, Mr. Jaffe. I also took an English class, math, and music classes.

The music courses at the university led me to get involved with the chorus, which sang songs in different languages. We learned to sing songs in Italian, German, and Spanish. Our teacher, Miss Gininne, did not respect or particularly care for me and two other students, who sang in outside bands.

The boy's last name was Perry and the girl's last name was Barnard. Miss Gininne felt that the songs we were singing weren't really music and that the only real music was classical. According to her, if you were not involved in classical music, you weren't involved at all. But we never let her attitude towards us affect our studying with the chorus.

While other students were studying, I was trying to figure out how to take advantage of someone and get something for nothing. I was still playing games and had not matured at all.

I was always trying to con people out of what they had, and I became very good at it. I knew what people, especially women, wanted, and I played the game until I got what I wanted and I would just toss them aside. I was a very cruel, cold, and calculating person. The hurt and pain that I felt was sometimes overwhelming, and my rage was directed at any and everyone.

To make matters worse, on the evening of September 18, 1971 I received the shocking news that my favorite Cousin Wayne Brooks who had just celebrated his twenty third birthday had been killed in a tragic car accident. Wayne was on his way home and was less than five miles from his house when the accident occurred. I had lost my closest cousin and one of my best friends and the grief that I felt was overwhelming. At that moment I thought that I was also going to die.

Wayne Brooks
(Photo courtesy of Carl Brooks)

CHAPTER 4:
DOWNHILL SLIDE

School and studying were just not for me, and I became very frustrated and decided to quit the University of Massachusetts. I left the U Mass after a year and a half and started working at U.S. Steel and as a bouncer at a nightclub on weekends.

My second job after leaving the university was at the "Nazareth Home for Boys." Nazareth was a group home for emotionally disturbed boys and was located in Leicester, Massachusetts. Nazareth sat on fifty-two acres of land, which included a swimming pool, a full basketball court, swings, and two Shetland ponies. The atmosphere at the school was upper middle class.

The housing for the boys was fairly new and consisted of four houses joined together with small hallways. Each house was equipped to handle nine children and there were children of different ages in each house. Each house had wall-to-wall carpeting and color televisions.

The nuns were considered to be the house mothers and would do all of the cooking, cleaning, and ironing, and they took care of the boys.

The counselors would act as mentors for the boys and give them guidance and structure. They would also take them out to various social events such as high school and college ball games, and professional games such as the Celtics, Patriot, or Red Sox games. The expense for those outings was usually sponsored by area charitable organizations such as the Kiwanis Club, Lions Club, and other civic organizations. The different organizations would also sponsor the boys at Christmas time. The boys were usually given an abundance of toys, clothing, and other needed items.

There was a diverse mixture of boys at the school. Some of the boys had no parents, some had parents who were not involved in their lives at all, and others had parents who were very involved.

The children were being conditioned to be responsive in an upper middle-class environment. Once they could do so for a specified length of time, they would then be released back to their families (if they had families). Ninety-nine percent of the time, the boys were released back into low-income, ghetto settings.

Some of the boys had a very difficult time when it was time to leave the school and return home. They did not want to return home to their previous life of poverty, as they knew what they had at the school as opposed to home. At the school they had three good square meals a day, proper hygiene, structure, education, and training. These times were very disruptive for the boys, and they would sometimes act out to prevent being sent back into their previous environment.

I really enjoyed working at Nazareth and I was very happy with my position. I even gave up working with the band due to my work schedule. I had to be on the job daily from 2:00 p.m. to midnight and Saturdays from noon until midnight.

I started working in a newly created position as a counselor for boys between the ages of fourteen and seventeen. Some of the children had been in the program since they were very young, but they had to leave when they became eighteen years of age.

My job was to help them get prepared to deal with the public, as they were not accustomed to getting out in public very often. They were schooled at the facility and most of them lacked social skills. I was responsible for teaching them how to complete employment applications and how to conduct themselves at an interview.

I would go to area companies, explain who I was and what I was trying to accomplish, and solicit their help. I would then go back to the school and set up mock interviews with the boys. The boys were taught how to sit up straight, how to look the interviewer in the eyes when speaking, how to think things out, not to stutter when answering questions, to shake hands firmly, the importance of dressing neatly, cleanliness, smiling, how to appear pleasant, how to sound interesting, how to ask questions about the job, as well as to how to answer questions they may be asked, and how to conduct themselves overall.

I also did research and taught classes on how to handle sexual situations and drug abuse. I also assisted some of the young men in getting their driver's license in order to become truck or cab drivers.

I would also take some of the boys to the area teen clubs to expose them to music. I would teach them how to approach the people and young ladies at the club, because they had not been exposed to this type of environment before.

One thing that I could not teach the boys was how to dance. The reason that I could not teach the boys how to dance was because I didn't know how to dance myself. I never learned to dance, because of a negative experience that I had had as a child around nine years of age.

I had prepared to the best of my ability for a couple of weeks, dancing in front of a mirror, so that I could ask a young lady to dance at a party I was going to attend. I had a crush on this young lady and when I approached her at the party and asked her to dance, she said, "No." That totally crushed me, and I never tried to dance again until I was about twenty-eight.

At the age of twenty-eight, I met someone whom I knew would not put up with my not dancing when we went out to the clubs; therefore, I knew that I would have to try dancing again.

There had been several small fires at the boy's home, because some of the boys would get their hands on matches and would sneak and smoke. When they would see the nuns, an adult, or a counselor coming, they would carelessly throw the cigarette down and run off.

Because this had happened a few times, I approached Father Tinsley, the Catholic priest who was in charge of running the home, and suggested a plan that might help alleviate the problem. I thought that if we could contact the parents of the boys that we knew were smoking and get them to a meeting, we would have them sign written authorizations giving the boys permission to smoke. Once the permission was given, we would then supervise the boys out on the basketball court while they smoked.

I quickly gained the confidence and respect of most of the adults and children at the home. We all had an excellent rapport, and the boys would always listen to my instructions without arguments.

We were instructed never to discipline the boys physically or handle them in a violent way. Even if we got into an altercation with the boys, we were never to physically discipline them. I was always able to talk to the boys and get them to calm down, but it was noted that some of the counselors did kick and hit the boys. I personally witnessed some incidents of abuse to the boys and was told by other counselors about other incidents of abuse that had occurred.

There was one counselor at the school who was envious of my tactics in handling the boys and he sought to discredit me with Father Tinsley and the staff.

One day while working at the school, I was called into the head office by Father Tinsley. Father Tinsley advised me that one of the counselors had accused me of stealing ping-pong balls.

Ping-pong balls, costing almost nothing at the time, were not something that I would even consider stealing, as I did not play the game and had no use for the balls.

I never played ping-pong with the boys at all; I did not even know how to play the game. I played pool, cards, board games, basketball; catch outside with the boys, baseball, and other games, but never ping-pong.

I stated to Father Tinsley, "I will stay here in the office, and I would appreciate it if you would go ask the boys in all four houses if I ever played ping-pong with them." Father Tinsley honored my request and went to each boy to inquire about whether or not I had ever played ping-pong with them. Father Tinsley returned to the office and apologized to me for the accusation, but would not tell me from whom it came. I asked Father Tinsley why he would take time out to accuse me, but would not take time out to tell me who my accuser was. I did not think that it was very fair, and I advised Father Tinsley that if he was not willing to tell me who had accused me and have the issue resolved in front of him, I would tender my resignation. Father Tinsley refused to allow me the opportunity to face my accuser, and at that point I resigned my position.

After a few years I joined another band as a solo singer for a short period of time, but did not really enjoy being the only lead singer. I was very nervous standing alone in front of a crowd.

I stopped singing after just a few months and returned to work at U.S. Steel and continued to work as a bouncer at the nightclub on weekends.

That same year, I accompanied my friend Scottie to the Worcester City Hospital to have a cyst removed. While he was being waited on by the doctor, I decided to apply for a job there. I applied for an orderly job and was hired.

As part of my duties as an orderly, I was required to pick up the dead bodies and their personal belongings and take them to the morgue. It was very difficult for me initially, as I would always get sick to my stomach when I went to the morgue and would regurgitate my lunch. This lasted for awhile and one day, I just got tired of spending money and not being able to keep my lunch down. I decided that day that I would bring my lunch and go down to the morgue to eat it. I would sit outside the morgue door and eat my lunch while the doctor was performing his work. I could see everything that was going on in the morgue through the glass in the door, and it was not pretty.

It wasn't long before I started getting complaints from the doctor performing the autopsies; he wanted to know how I could sit there and eat while he was performing his work. I explained to the doctor what had gotten me to that point, but I was asked to cease the practice of eating my lunch in the morgue area.

In 1972 at the age of twenty-one, while working at the hospital, I met Barbara Jaspon, a twenty-two-year-old LPN on the floor where I worked as an orderly.

Barbara was a Polish/Italian woman who lived with her Italian mother and Polish father. Barbara's father was a police officer with the City of Worcester.

I really had not paid any attention to Barbara until she started making advances and remarks to me while at work. I finally asked some of my coworkers about her, and they thought that she was a pretty decent lady.

I then started talking with Barbara and found that we appeared to have a lot in common. Barbara and I agreed to start dating outside of the hospital, but we had to keep our relationship private.

At the same time I decided that I wanted to give up the street life, settle down, and become a man. I thought that part of being a man was to be married and have a family. I liked Barbara a lot, but I don't think that I was ever truly in love with her. I had known Barbara for about one month when I one day said, "Hey, how about us getting married?" and she said, "Fine."

From the beginning of our relationship, Barbara's family, including her aunt, who was the charge nurse on my floor, did not approve of our dating or the relationship.

Barbara's aunt made it very difficult for me to work at the hospital. I could not do anything right in her sight. I received one complaint after another from her, and things got so bad that I had to quit the job.

Barbara and I continued to see each other and got married within one month of meeting. Barbara and I got married secretly at the Justice of the Peace office, and I thought that all of my dreams had finally come true.

All that I ever dreamed of and wanted in life was a loving and peaceful home environment, a job, a saved Christian wife, children, and someone to love me forever and never leave me alone.

I rented an apartment for Barbara and me and borrowed money from my father to purchase furniture. Barbara was still living with her parents at the time and had not told them that we were married. I had the apartment for a month and Barbara still had not moved in with me.

I confronted Barbara about not letting her parents know that we were married, and she stated that she would need more time to find the right moment to tell them because she knew that they would not approve.

I waited another week and Barbara still had not told her parents. At that point I became very impatient and I took it upon myself to go to Barbara's parents and let them know that we were married. I wanted my wife to come and live with me or I would have to get a roommate to help pay the expenses for the apartment.

I arrived at the Jaspon's home all ready for a fight. Their German shepherd dog was in the front yard, but I just stepped right over him, daring him to move with my actions. I was ready for anything that might come my way.

I knocked on the door and when Mr. and Mrs. Jaspon came to the door, I told them that there was something that they needed to know. I advised them that Barbara and I were married and that I wanted her to come home to live with me at our apartment. Barbara's father walked away and went into another room and returned with a pistol. At that point I advised him that he was not the only one with a gun, and I would not hesitate to use it. At that point, Mr. Jaspon asked me to leave his property and I did; I felt that my mission had been accomplished.

I didn't know what happened after I left, but the following week Barbara and her seventeen-year-old sister Judy came to our apartment to live. Barbara's father had put both of the girls out of his home. Barbara was put out for marrying me, and her sister was put out for supporting her.

Judy caused a lot of problems after moving in with us. She met my friend (who was a married man) and they started dating. Barbara and I both agreed that it was not the right thing to do, so we gave Judy an ultimatum: to stop seeing him or get out. Judy continued to see my friend and eventually left our apartment with him. Judy and my friend lived on the streets for a while, but eventually the two of them got jobs and got an apartment together. My friend finally got a divorce from his wife, which caused a lot of confusion, as it usually does, and he and Judy later married. Since then both of them have passed away with brain cancer.

My dream life with Barbara was short-lived. Barbara and I started to have problems almost immediately. Barbara was a very cruel woman and would say or do things to make me feel bad or hurt my feelings.

I was already feeling insecure about my sexuality, and Barbara started to make fun of me and joked about me. She did not appear to have any feelings for me sexually and never wanted to be close to me. I can't say that it was her fault entirely, because I really didn't know how to be a husband and show love to my wife. We just sort of existed together in the same house.

I really wanted to have lots of children to compensate for the family that I had longed for, but never had; I was concerned when Barbara did not conceive.

Barbara and I talked about what was happening, and we decided to see a doctor to find out if there was a problem. We made the appointment with the doctor and had tests done to see why we were not getting pregnant. When the test results were received, it was not good news. The test results showed that my sperm count was very low, and the doctor advised us that it would be next to impossible for me to father a child. This news was devastating to me because I had always dreamed of having a house full of children. I didn't want to believe or accept this news, and I asked the doctor to have a second test done in case a mistake had been made on the first test; the second test came back with the same results.

The relationship between Barbara and I became more strained; we would separate and reconcile often.

During one of our numerous separations, I caught Barbara making out in a car with another man. She didn't appear to care that I saw her and continued kissing the man; I was very hurt, but I didn't want her to see my tears.

We separated once because Barbara had gotten involved with taking a lot of different drugs, which we had agreed that we would not do.

One morning Barbara came into the kitchen to get her pocketbook. When she grabbed for her pocketbook, everything fell out of it, and I noticed that she had lots of drugs and different pills. I confronted her about the drugs because we had agreed that we both would smoke marijuana, but that we would not get involved with any other type of drugs. I told her that I was not going to be a part of that. When I tried to talk with Barbara about the drugs in her purse, she grabbed the purse and the pills and ran out of the apartment.

Shortly after Barbara left my father called me from the hospital and told me that my mother had had a stroke. He told me that my mother was paralyzed and was not talking. This was quite a jolt and was very frightening to me. My marriage to Barbara was in major trouble and now my mother was sick; I was devastated.

My mother stayed in the hospital for two weeks before she could speak and move her limbs a little. My mother was sent home with orders for a visiting nurse and an aide to come in daily to cook, clean, and help her out.

My mother was improving well and we thought that she was on the road to a good recovery. She was walking with help, but one day while being supported by the nurse, she slipped, but did not fall. The episode frightened her so badly that she refused to attempt to walk again.

During one of our many separations, Barbara called and announced to me that she was pregnant. From the beginning I had doubts that I had fathered the child and questioned Barbara about it. I reminded her about the tests that we had taken and the doctor's statement that I would never be able to father a child. Barbara insisted that she had not been sexually involved with anyone since our last separation and that the child could only be mine.

As I pointed out, I did not have a good beginning coming into this world, and I did not know who I was really connected to biologically, and I didn't need to be lied to about this child.

I told Barbara that we were still friends and that I would continue to help her. I would also do what I could for the child, but if the child was not mine biologically, I needed to know the truth. Barbara was adamant about telling me that it was my child. She assured me that there was no way that it could not be my child, and she wanted to come back home and have us raise our child together as a family.

I really wanted to believe Barbara about the child, because I wanted children very badly, but deep down inside I knew better. I thought about it for a while and I made a conscious decision to accept the child as my own, even though I knew in my heart that it was not true.

Barbara and I reconciled again and got another apartment together. Things were going well for the next few months. We were very

(Photo courtesy of Robert Johnston)

happy planning for the birth of our first child, and I attended childbirth classes with Barbara.

On September 18, 1976, our baby girl Nicole was born. I was very happy to be a father, and loved and cared for Nicole as though she was my very own. I never thought of her as being another man's child; she was mine in every sense of the word.

I enjoyed shopping for clothing for Nicole; I loved to see her dressed up. I would take care of Nicole when I arrived home from work and enjoyed every moment that I spent with her; we had a very close relationship from the very beginning.

One Friday night Barbara went out and did not return home until about 3:00 a.m. I opened my eyes and looked up at her and saw that her clothes and hair were in a mess. Her clothes were in disarray and her hair was standing all over her head.

I knew then that Barbara was back in the streets using drugs. After seeing her in that condition, in disgust, I just rolled over and went back to sleep.

One Saturday morning around 11:00 a.m., I was sitting in the kitchen reading my newspaper and Barbara was in a hurry to leave. I asked her where she was going, and she said that she was going to the store to pick up something. I asked her what she needed to pick up because two days before, on Thursday, we had gone shopping and gotten everything we needed, including commodities that would last us for a month. We had picked up food, aluminum foil, you name it, we had it; we did not need anything.

Barbara just kept saying, "I've got to go, I've got to go," and she was acting very nervous. In that case I told her to take Nicole with her, as I had kept her the night before while she was out. Barbara ignored my request and rushed out of the door leaving Nicole in the apartment with me again.

While Barbara was out, a collect telephone call came in for her. I asked the operator where the call originated and she stated, "Framingham, Massachusetts." I accepted the call because Barbara had been looking for another nursing job and had applied at a hospital in Framingham. Barbara wanted to change jobs because the hospitals closer to Boston paid much more money than the hospitals in Worcester.

I accepted the call and a young man asked to speak with Barbara. I stated, "Barbara is not in at the moment. I am her husband; if there is anything I can help you with, just let me know."

The man responded, "All you can do is let me kick your black ass." It turns out that this was the man that she had been out with the night before.

I said to the man, "Since you know my unlisted telephone number and must also know where I live, then if you think that you need to kick my ass, then come on over here and do it. I don't have to fight over her, and you don't have to try and kick my ass; that's not necessary: You can have her."

When Barbara returned home I told her what had taken place. She got very angry and started throwing ashtrays and different things at me.

At that point, I took my things and left. I stayed at my parents' apartment for about three weeks, and then I rented my own apartment.

I never looked back at Barbara as far as a relationship was concerned, but I did take care of my responsibilities towards Nicole. I was supposed to get Nicole every other week, but I usually picked her up every week. I continued to buy all of her clothes, paid child support, and provided her with all of the necessities.

Barbara decided that she no longer wanted to be in the apartment so she moved in with her sister Judy and Judy's boyfriend. Judy and her boyfriend were living in a housing project in the Green Brooke Valley area.

I continued to pick Nicole up weekly for about nine months. I called one day to let Barbara know that I was picking Nicole up and the telephone had been disconnected. I drove out to Framingham and learned that Barbara had moved and was nowhere to be found. I tried to locate her sister without success, and no one appeared to know anything about their whereabouts.

I waited for several weeks and still did not hear from Barbara. I then went to my attorney and he filed papers with the courts to try and find where my child support payments were going and try to locate Barbara and Nicole. I was really concerned because I knew that Barbara was back on drugs, and I did not know their whereabouts or what might have happened to them.

In hopes of locating them, a court-ordered paternity test date was set up for Barbara, Nicole, and me, but Barbara did not show up for the appointment.

Eventually I was called in by the courts, and they cancelled my child support obligation due to default by Barbara. I was absolved of all responsibility in the case. Family Services advised me that they were getting back cancelled checks from different banks up and down the East Coast.

Family Services, who now had control of the case, were trying to force Barbara to come in so that they could locate her and find out the condition of Nicole. They wanted to make sure that she was being properly cared for and was in a safe environment.

About eight and a half years later, the Family Court contacted me and informed me that Barbara and Nicole had returned to the Massachusetts area and that I had a good chance of getting full custody of Nicole. They stated that Barbara had a court case pending that could possibly result in her going to prison.

I asked them why it had taken so long for them to get in contact with me and they stated that they did not know where I was. I told them that they were lying, because I was still working at my same job with the City of Worcester Fire Department. They could have easily checked where I was through my Social Security number. I was working with the Fire Department when they left and I was still working there.

I passed all of the information along to my attorney and he advised me how to handle the matter. The attorney advised me to provide a secure place with supervision where I could meet with Nicole until she felt comfortable being alone with me. Nicole was a baby when she was taken away and she did not remember me. I did as I was instructed and started having supervised visits with her, but this did not last very long.

Nicole appeared disinterested in visiting with me and totally stopped coming. I really didn't understand what happened and why Nicole did not want to visit with me. I tried to make the visits as comfortable as possible, and I even allowed Barbara's two other children to come along on the visits. Barbara had had two more children after we separated and after she left Worcester. I always had lots of activities planned and I thought that the children always enjoyed themselves.

At the time I could only speculate that Barbara was discouraging Nicole from visiting with me, and it was not until years later that I learned the truth.

When Nicole was older, I again tried to have a relationship with her, because she was starting to get into trouble with the law and I wanted to help her. She was very hostile towards me, and she finally confided in me that her mother had told her things about me that made her afraid of me. I tried to explain to Nicole that what Barbara had told her was not the truth, but it really did not help the relationship.

Barbara had told Nicole that I was gay in order to make her dislike me, and I also realized that Barbara had told Nicole that I was not her biological father.

The relationship between Nicole and me did not work out at all. Nicole continued to get into trouble. She ended up getting pregnant and had a son (who I have never seen). She finally ended up in prison for assaulting and robbing an elderly woman.

CHAPTER 5:
SECOND CHANCE

In 1976 I took tests to become a police officer and a firefighter. I passed both tests. I was looking forward to working with juveniles in the Police Department, but I was turned down for that position. I was offered a position as a narcotics officer, but I had to refuse the position, as I could not rat on my friends with whom I had spent all of my teenage years on the streets committing crimes. There was a bond there that I could not break. I wanted to help young people to avoid getting into gangs and trouble in the first place, but that was not to be.

A few years after turning down the narcotics officer job and accepting the firefighter position with the City of Worcester Fire Department, I had the opportunity to speak with Police Chief Thomas Lawrence Lahey, II, who owed me a favor. I saved his son, Thomas Lawrence Lahey, III, from a terrible beating when we were attending Chandler Street Junior. High School, which was in an affluent Jewish neighborhood. The incident with his son took place at school.

Thomas III was a very humorous, funny kind of kid. One day I came outside for lunch and noticed a bunch of kids surrounding him. I went over to see what was going on and the kids were threatening to kick his butt. I knew that Thomas III was not a fighter and couldn't defend himself, so I told the kids to fight me and leave Thomas alone.

I started fighting with a couple of the kids and the others ran away. The teachers and staff came outside and broke up the fight. Thomas III told his father what had happened and how I had saved him from a beating, and they invited me to come to their house that weekend.

I went over to his house and met his mother and father (and a sister, I think). Chief Lahey thanked me for saving his son from a beating; he appreciated what I had done because he recognized that his son was not a fighter.

He stated that he was sorry if I got into any trouble, which I didn't, because there were plenty of witnesses that explained what happened to the principal.

The Chief again thanked me and told me if there was ever anything that he could do for me, to let him know because he felt indebted to me. That was the end of that story.

The chief advised me that I should have gotten in contact with him, and he would have made sure that I was hired in the position working with juveniles with the Police Department. But I guess that it just was not meant to be.

In 1977 I went to work with the City of Worcester as a firefighter in the water company. At that time the Fire Department had four divisions: the water company, the ladder company, scopes, and an emergency squad.

There were only three black firefighters at the station where I was assigned, and the rest were whites and other races.

Shortly after being hired at the Fire Department, my father became very ill, but he hid his condition from the family for several years.

By this time both of my parents were getting up in age and were already having major health problems.

My father finally told me that he had been diagnosed with prostate and bone cancer. He had struggled with the illness for years, but kept it to himself. He stated that I should not worry because he had taken care of it. By that statement I was under the impression that he had gotten the necessary medical treatment and that he would be okay.

But one day he was in so much pain that he called for me to come over and asked me to call the ambulance to take him to the hospital. When I arrived at the house my father handed me his keys and told me to take care of the house and pay his bills while he was gone. He was laughing and joking with me, and I wasn't overly concerned about him or his condition. I stayed at home with my mother, who was confined to a wheelchair, while the ambulance transported my father to the hospital.

I had planned to go to the hospital later that day after getting someone to stay with my mother.

About an hour after the ambulance had picked up my father, the doctor called and stated that my father was in a coma and advised me that he would not recover. The doctor advised me that the family should come to the hospital if they wanted to see my father alive again. I thought about what the doctor had said for awhile before

I decided to tell my mother what the doctor had said about his condition.

I could not believe that my father was in a coma and would not be returning home. I couldn't bear the thought of seeing my father in that condition; I wanted to remember him as the big, strong, and strapping man that he was.

I finally got up enough courage to tell my mother about my father's condition and how I felt about seeing him. I told my mother that I did not want to remember my father in a coma and I had decided not to go to the hospital. I asked my mother if she would have any bad feelings towards me if I did not go to the hospital, and she said, "No." My mother was very understanding and supportive of me. She repeated, "No, Bobbie, it's okay; I understand."

Some of my mother's friends and church members helped her to get to the hospital each day so that she could be with her husband in his last days.

My father remained in the coma for nine days before he finally passed away on February 8, 1982.

Uncle Paul, Aunt Flossie, Cousin Lawrence, and other relatives drove up from North Carolina for my father's funeral. They stopped in Washington, DC, to pick up another nephew who also wanted to attend the funeral.

My mother and I were very happy to know that so many of our relatives cared enough to come all the way from North Carolina to Massachusetts to attend my father's funeral. It was more like a family reunion than a funeral. Immediately after the funeral, all of the relatives had to return home for work and there was a great sense of loss and loneliness.

I returned to work at the Fire Department and struggled to adjust to no longer having my father in my life.

It was not long before dissention arose between me and the Fire Chief. The issue was two hand-drawn pictures, one of which was of a black man. These pictures were passed around to each Fire Department designating new requirements for hair and moustache cuts.

The hand-drawn picture of the black man was drawn with crossed eyes and negative features, while the hand-drawn picture of the white man was as it should have been: nice and neat.

The majority of the firefighters were taken aback by this. We could not understand why the Fire Chief permitted this to happen since he had to approve the pictures being passed around.

I talked with my fellow firefighters, and we all agreed to take our grievances to management. We requested a meeting with the Chief to discuss our complaint regarding the pictures.

When the meeting was held with the Fire Chief I was the only one who spoke up immediately and stated my position. Everyone else was quiet and later stated that they were afraid of losing their jobs.

At the meeting, the Chief initially denied having anything to do with the drawings, but we knew that that was a lie. The Spanish and black men that attended the meeting started questioning the Chief about the drawings, but I was the main person speaking out. I cornered the Chief a few times with his answers, and he became very frustrated with me. The Chief became very angry with me; his face turned red and his vocal tone changed.

After that meeting, the Chief appeared to carry a grudge against me for the position that I had put him in, but I felt that I had done what was necessary to maintain our dignity as men as well as minorities.

After being with the Fire Department for approximately four years, there was a potential for me to move into fire prevention. At that point, I started putting in my applications to apply for the position with the Chief, who was in charge of hiring. Each time a promotion came up I would apply, but I would always be overlooked, and a white person would be hired even though I was more qualified for the position.

I have never been one to set back and accept injustice, so I approached the Chief with my concerns. I told him that I had copies of every application that I had sent to him requesting a promotion, and all of it had been well documented. I advised him that if he should pass me over one more time without giving me a chance, I would be going to see my attorney to sign and date an affidavit that had already been drawn up for me to sue him, the Fire Department, and the City.

Shortly after my meeting with the Chief, I became ill with a bad case of food poisoning. While I was out on medical leave, a Fire Inspector position was posted. One of my fellow firefighters called to advise me of the posting and advised me to get my application in, because the posting would be closing out in a few days.

It was my feeling, but I had no proof, that the posting was deliberately put up while I was out sick to prevent me from applying. But fortunately, by my friend's call, I was able to apply for and get promoted to the Fire Inspector position.

I was in my new position as a Fire Inspector for about one year when the Chief summoned me to his office. My initial thought was, "Now what! What's going on? What have I done?" I went to the Chief's office and took a seat.

The Chief stated that something had happened that had never happened before, at least while he was Chief. Now I'm really getting nervous, because I couldn't figure out what I had done. The Chief then opened up a folder and pulled out two letters that had been written by two people who I had visited and inspected their homes. The letters turned out to be statements of gratitude to me for helping these people bring their homes up to code. They were commenting on how courteous I was, how helpful I was, how much of a gentleman I was, and how nice it was to know that this caliber of person is representing our city.

I always tried to help everyone, especially the older people. I would help them put up their smoke detectors or alarms, or anything they needed.

The Chief apologized to me and stated that if he had any misconceptions about me, they were now gone. He said, "Go on back out there and continue to do the good job that you are doing."

I was able to advance to the rank of Firefighter Inspector over the twelve-year period which I was employed with the department.

During my tenure with the City of Worcester Fire Department, I continued to have turmoil in my life.

Then in 1980 I met Dorothy (whom we called "Dot"), a beautiful black woman from the Durham, North Carolina, area. Dot was living in Worcester at the time with her six children. Dot had three girls, Darlene, Dawn, and Debra and three boys, David, Darnell, and Darrin. It did not matter to me that she had six children; it was attractive to me, because I always enjoyed the idea of having lots of children around.

I wanted Dot and I just felt like I had to have her. I was not in love with Dot, but I loved her. By now I didn't know how to really love.

Dot thought that I had lots of money and continually asked me when we were getting married. I tried to explain to Dot that I did not have any money; I was just a poor working man, but she was convinced otherwise. My job at the Fire Department paid well, but it did not make me rich by any stretch of the imagination.

Dot and I dated for almost a year before she finally convinced me that we should get married. Once I had made up my mind to marry Dot, I single-handedly planned the wedding within two weeks.

Dot and I had a pretty large wedding. Dot's family came up from North Carolina, and all of her family from the Worcester area attended the wedding. The wedding was very nice, and we all enjoyed ourselves very much.

At a certain point, two of Dot's sons David and Darnell stopped going to school and were not working or helping out at home. I discussed the matter with Dot and told her that if the boys were not going to go to school, they had to go to work and help out around the house. I told her that I refused to support that type of situation; I had no problem supporting them as long as they were doing what they were required to do. I would not support them if they were just eating, sleeping, and hanging out. It got to the point where they were coming in at 3:00 a.m., being disruptive, and disturbing my sleep. I asked her to get a handle on this situation, because I had to be up and at the Fire Department by 7:30 a.m., and I was not able to get my proper rest.

I purchased a new pine dinette set for the family. I came home one evening to find the oldest boy David sitting with his dirty boots propped up on one of the chairs. It had been snowing and there was lots of salt and grit from the walkway on his boots. I asked him to take his boots off of the chair, and he responded by asking, "Why don't you get a life?"

I called Dot in and asked her to intervene with her son, and she said that she did not want to get in the middle of what was going on. I informed her that once she invited me into her home, she was already in the middle of it, and I had previously asked her to get some control over the boys and the situation, but she had not done so.

Dot refused to say anything. I told her that since I was not being shown any respect in the household, and she was permitting her grown sons to tell me to kiss their ass and go to hell, I would stop contributing to the household. I told her that I would be putting money in the bank, and one of two things was going to happen.

First, I would save up enough money to get my own apartment and I would move out, or second, she would gain control over the situation to my satisfaction.

If she wanted me to stay, then she would show me by getting control of her sons so that we could all live there together in peace. I was not asking that anyone be put out; I was simply asking that if the boys weren't going to attend school that they get jobs, contribute to the household, and become the men that they thought they were. Needless to say, none of my requests were granted; things remained the same.

Dot and I fought constantly about her children, who were disrespectful and out of control. Things got so bad between us that the name-calling started. Dot really tried to hurt me as much as she could when we argued. She would always bring up the fact that I was not as well-endowed as other men and ridiculed me about my sensitive nature and how easily I cried when upset.

Before leaving for work one morning, Dot and I argued again about the boys and their attitudes. When I returned home from work that afternoon, Dot had set my belongings outside of the door.

I took my belongings to my parents' home temporarily, until I was able to get my own apartment.

That incident marked the end of my marriage to Dot, but she and I remained friendly and would talk and continued to interact with one another, but we never reconciled.

Dot and I were married for four difficult years before we finally divorced in 1984.

One day I was going up some steps to inspect a house, when I slipped on some wet leaves and fell. My knee was severely injured when I hit the steps. My knee locked up and I could not straighten out my leg. I had torn cartilages and sustained several bruises on my knee.

My doctor tried to treat me with physical therapy, but it did not work. He then suggested laser surgery, which I underwent. The doctor advised me that I should be able to return to work in a couple of weeks. He also referred me to a physical therapist that put my knee through exercises, which were too strenuous. The physical therapy was causing me more pain and discomfort and was discontinued when my doctor realized what was happening.

I was out of work for several months and had to use a walking cane to get around.

After I had been out for a while, I received a letter from the Fire Chief telling me that I needed to return to work, quit, or be fired, and he gave me a deadline date to do so. Realizing that I had exhausted my medical leave and had no attorney, I requested permission from my doctor to return to work, and I went back even though my knee had not completely healed and was still bothering me.

Later on, Dot and I became very close again when her second oldest son Darnell had to have a heart transplant. I knew that she would need the support, and I was there for her. I would take her to the hospital in Boston to visit with her son and was just there for her. When her son got out of the hospital, he started going to church and appeared to have a different view on life. Prior to having the heart transplant, he had spent some time in jail as he had gotten into some trouble.

One night Darnell was at a party, not doing anything wrong, but was shot in the heart and killed by a young man from the Boston area. The shooting occurred because the young man from Boston wanted Darnell's gold chain and he refused to give it to him.

The young man from Boston left the party, returned with a gun, opened the door, and shot Dot's son Darnell in the chest.

On the day of Darnell's funeral, his sister Dawn did not want to go the grave site for the final committal, but I convinced her to go in order to bring closure. I told her that she would be sorry and regret it later if she did not go to say her final "Good-Byes" to her brother. I continued to plead with Dawn and she eventually changed her mind and went to the grave site. She later hugged me and thanked me for convincing her to go.

I supported Dot as much as I could during that time, but we eventually went our separate ways.

I continued to communicate with Dot and some of her children, who loved me and thanked me for what I tried to do for the family; they continued calling me Dad and stayed in contact with me.

The loss of another family and other events sent my life into another downhill spiral. At this point I decided that I hated women, and I would just use them and throw them away (as they had thrown me away).

From that point on I had no more meaningful relationships with women. I would get involved with women, but the relationships would only last for a few months before I was ready to move on. I used women to help support my expensive habits for years. The relationships were always good in the beginning, but in the end, there was always the issue of my sexuality.

I became involved more and more with illegal drugs and at one point in my life I did not leave my apartment for five years except to go to work. I had no friends and no interest in life or living. I would shoot up daily with heroin and barely had enough money to buy food. Sometimes I would not eat at all for days. My life appeared to be hopeless, and I finally attempted to commit suicide, because I felt that I had nothing to live for.

I had tried everything that I knew how to secure love, a home, and a family, but I had always failed. I couldn't even succeed at committing suicide.

I started questioning why God was keeping me here. I needed to know, because I was in so much pain and I needed help.

I decided to turn my life over to God; I was desperate to be saved. I remembered my upbringing and how my mother had conducted prayer services in our home. I tried to draw strength from God and his word.

One day a Caucasian friend of mine that I had known in high school came to the door selling life insurance. While he was there, he asked me about my salvation and if I was attending church.

I told him that I was not saved and really had not thought about attending church since I was a teenager. My friend was heavily involved in church and invited me to attend his church, which was about a ten-minute walk from my apartment. I decided that I would take him up on his offer and start attending church.

The church congregation basically was all white except for me and Brother James Marshall. I also found out that one of the lieutenants at the Fire Department was a minister at the church.

I had been attending the church for about a month, when on several occasions a young man approached me several times in the foyer of the church and kept asking, "Are you saved? Are you saved?" I didn't know how to answer him, because I didn't know what it meant to be saved.

As he attempted to explain salvation to me, some other people came over to us and started explaining to me what it meant to be saved. They asked me if I believed that Jesus existed, whether or not he was the son of God, whether Jesus came here for the purpose of being a living example, sacrificing his life on the cross, shedding his blood, and defeating Satan in hell those three days, and rose on the third day and ascended to Heaven and sat on the right hand of the Father. They said that if I truly believed that in my heart and was able to confess it publicly, then I would be saved. As I made my confession, they placed their hands on me and prayed for me. I attended the services that evening, but didn't really notice any specific change.

I went home, went to bed, and when I woke up the next morning, I definitely noticed a change in my spirit; I just felt different. I knew that there was something different and that a change had been made.

At that point Dot and I were living together, but we weren't married. We had already gotten a divorce, but we decided as friends to share the same apartment in order to help save on our monthly expenses. I asked Dot to attend church with me but she was not interested.

I continued to attend church regularly and sought out additional information on my salvation.

There came a time when the same person who introduced me to that church tried to dissuade me from attending. One of the things that he had spoken to me about when he came to my house selling insurance was having musical outlets in the church. After being at the church for a short period of time, I approached him about getting involved in music within the church. My friend was aware of my musical abilities and my playing with the band around the general area. His response was, "Well, maybe you can go to another church in Boston. They have a choir, a lot of good singers, and you would probably like their choir much better. Why don't you check them out?"

At that point I felt hurt; I thought that he was trying to push me away because he didn't want me to become a part of their singing venue. I didn't know what the situation was, whether he was threatened by my vocal abilities or just didn't want a band member in the church group.

I was really enjoying attending that church and liked being there. The church that he directed me to go to in Boston was an all-black congregation called the House of Prayer No. 5.

I started attending the House of Prayer No. 5 and I was baptized for the remission of all of my sins. I came very close to the evidence of being filled with the Holy Spirit and speaking in tongues, but was highly distracted at the point that this was happening, because I had to go to work.

I was in Boston and had to return to Worcester, which was about one and a half hours travel time, and I was concentrating on not being late for work. I was working at the Fire Department on the evening shift, which started at 5:00 p.m., and it was already 3:00 p.m., and I didn't allow that spirit to manifest itself. I attended the church for about six to eight months before I backslid.

I started hanging out on the streets again, drinking and getting high. I stayed in that mode for a couple of years. I moved out of the apartment with Dot and got my own place again. I continued to do things that I should not have done for a while longer.

I eventually returned to church and joined Grace Community Church of God in Christ, which was headed by Rev. Black. This was a fairly new church congregation formed by Rev. Black. The gifts of the Spirit were very apparent at the church. I stayed at Grace Community Church of God in Christ for a couple of years and sang in the choir.

I became disenchanted with the pastor and the church when a false rumor started circulating about me and one of the young girls in the church. This young girl, who was originally from Boston, was living with one of the church families at the time. She was trying to get into the church in order to get off of the streets. She sang in the choir with me, she had a beautiful voice, and we would discuss music and singing. When she became pregnant, the rumor started circulating that I had impregnated her and was the father of the unborn child. I knew that I wasn't the father, as I had never even put my hands on the girl, and I didn't know whether she was female or male.

According to the information she had given to me, she had gotten impregnated by an Italian man living in Worcester. She then left the church; according to gossip, she was too embarrassed by the situation that she and I had created.

This rumor had gotten back to the pastor through a third party, and he did not like it and started shunning me. I approached the pastor with the intention of clearing up the rumor, but he was not receptive to me.

I went to the pastor one Sunday after church and told him that I was aware that something was between us, and I wanted the opportunity to sit down with him and tell him the truth so that we could get back to normal as far as our interaction with one another.

The pastor and I made an appointment to sit down and talk. I showed up for the appointment, but the pastor never came. I tried calling his home and got no answer, but I left a message letting him know that I was waiting for him at the church and that I would wait another forty-five minutes to an hour. The pastor did not show up or call and never acknowledged my telephone call.

The next Sunday at church, I again approached the pastor to acknowledge that we had not had our meeting. His response was,

"Yes that's true," and he never offered or attempted to reschedule our meeting.

Whether the rumors were true or not, I felt that the pastor did not want to squash them and find a resolution to our problems. Having that stigma hanging over my head by my pastor, who was supposed to be a leader of the church and myself, I felt that it would be best that I leave that congregation. I had reached out to the pastor trying to find a resolution, but he didn't appear to be interested, and there was nothing that I could do to fix the problem since I hadn't created it.

My mother was also very ill. After her stroke she was paralyzed and confined to a wheelchair. My mother did not have anyone in Worcester to take care of her after my father's death. At the time I was married, with six stepchildren, and was working with the Fire Department and was unable to care for her. We talked and my mother decided that she would move down South with her sister Flossie.

Aunt Janie Brooks, Cousin Lawrence Brooks, and his nephew came up to Worcester on the train to pick up my mother and took her back to North Carolina to live with Flossie.

After packing up my mother's personal effects, she and Aunt Janie flew back to North Carolina. Cousin Lawrence and his nephew rented a U-Haul Truck and drove back to North Carolina with my mother's belongings.

After getting my mother settled in North Carolina I had more freedom to concentrate on my music.

In 1985 Scottie and I formed another band called "Affirmation." We placed ads in the paper for band member try-outs. We held auditions and selected the people that we wanted to play in the band. We composed a seven-member band: two females and five males. One of the females played the keyboard, and the other sang strictly lead out front with Scottie and me.

We also had a saxophone player, a bass player, and a guitar player. We worked at several different nightclubs, performed weddings, and worked in the Worcester area. At one point the band members became disinterested in practicing and learning more songs, so at that point, I told Scottie that I would just drop out of the band. I dropped out of the band and did not sing with a group again until the early nineties.

I would visit with my mother in North Carolina as often as possible. Aunt Flossie would call often to keep me updated on my mother's health status. My mother's health continued to decline over the next year and a half, and at the age of seventy-seven her kidneys failed. My mother was admitted to the hospital and died within hours of her admission. She died on July 19, 1986, and was buried at the Ebenezer Baptist Church Cemetery in Kings Mountain.

The Ebenezer Baptist Church
(Photo courtesy of Jeanette Surratte)

I voluntarily left my job with the Fire Department in 1989, about three years after I had returned to work from medical leave due to my knee injury.

I was very depressed after losing my mother and felt that I needed a change in my environment. I felt completely alone and I felt that it would help me to be near my family.

I then moved to Baltimore in 1989 to be near my Cousin Inez and her husband Tonk. I had liked Baltimore since I was a child and wanted to live there. My parents would always stop in Baltimore on our way to North Carolina for vacation to visit with relatives living there. We would stop on the way down to North Carolina and stop again on our way back to Worcester.

Once in Baltimore, it was difficult for me to find a job; everything was downsizing and under sizing, and jobs were difficult to come by. I sent out approximately fifty resumes and personally went to about fifty businesses and telephoned numerous companies and could not secure a job. I was finally able to get a part-time job at a men's clothing store working at minimum wage.

I eventually returned to Worcester because I could not earn enough money to support myself in Baltimore.

Around 1992 I joined a do wop, a capella group that consisted of three policemen. Sam Bracey was one of the police officers, and he had a brother that we called "House," but his name was Charles Bracey. The other police officers were Eddie O'Connell and Charles Brace. The other members were Ricky Rangel and me. We sang together for a few years and the group disbanded.

While singing with this group I received more bad news from North Carolina.

I was notified that my Cousin Clyde Brooks had been killed on his job at the China Grove Mill in Gastonia on December 2, 1992. Clyde was killed when his shirt sleeve got caught in a machine in the textile mill. The machines in the mill were very loud and no one heard his cries for help. The machine pulled Clyde's arm off and he bleed to death before he was found lying on the floor. No one really knew exactly how the accident happened or how long Clyde had lain on the floor. Clyde's death left another void in my heart and life.

Cousin Clyde Brooks
(Photo courtesy of Josie Brooks)

I was working at the Fallon Clinic as a DME Technician in West Boylston, Massachusetts, when I saw a person whom I recognized as being one of my best friends, Luther Ward. I could not believe that he had retired from the military and was working for the same company in the same building.

Luther had retired from the Marines in 1995. In 1974, while he was in the Marines, Luther married his first wife Teresa, who was from the Philippines. Teresa had a son by the name of Anthony, and she had passed away.

Luther remarried on January 30, 1997, to Leonora, who was also from the Philippines, and she had a daughter by the name of Vanessa. Luther's wedding to Leonora took place at 5:15 p.m., and she died on the same day, hours later, at the San Bernardino Hospital in California from cardiac arrest.

Luther was going through a very difficult time in his life; he was very angry and I tried to be there for him. He was a very wild man when he was in the military, but he had really changed and settled down since his wife's death.

Luther finally enrolled in anger management classes to help him get through the trauma of losing his first and second wives. He related to me that he learned a lot about himself and others in the classes. One thing that stood out for him was how some of the participants described their childhood and the abuse that they endured. It made him think about how blessed he was to be raised in the Clayton and Laurel Streets neighborhood, where everyone cared for one another.

At one point, Luther's family and friends were really afraid for him because he was so depressed. In order to help him, they decided to introduce him to Leonora. This lady had the same name as his second wife and was also from the Philippines.

Luther and Leonora had three children: two sons, Charlie and Luther A. D. Ward IV, and one daughter, Alexandra. Charlie was born in February 1996, Luther IV was born (with cerebral palsy) in 1998, and Alexandra was born January 20, 2001.

Luther and I spent a lot of time together talking and supporting one another, and we hung out like two settled-down old men. I would go over to Luther's house and visit with him and his family, and he would come to my apartment. Every Thursday night, Luther and I would go out to eat dinner, and he would always bring one of his three children along with him.

Luther had really settled down and became a real family man, and he was sort of a loner. Luther had always told me that he would never leave his family like his father had left him and his siblings.

When I was in Baltimore, and decided to move back to Worcester, Luther took the train down to Baltimore and drove the U-Haul Truck back to Worcester for me. We talked about everything and we knew that we could trust one another.

Luther was really brilliant with computers, and he helped me learn how to operate one and how to download and record music. We discussed going on trips together, and we really wanted to go to the Philippines but I did not have a birth certificate, which was required to get my passport.

CHAPTER 6:
ANOTHER TURN

July of 2000, when I was around forty-nine years old, I was contacted by a woman claiming to be one of my siblings. This lady informed me that my biological mother was in the hospital and that she was very ill. She stated that the doctor's had given our mother up and had requested that the family be called in.

Up until that point, I had no idea that I even had siblings, and this was a shock to me.

According to this lady I had three half brothers (one was deceased), and two sisters including herself. She proceeded to tell me that she had put forth a tremendous amount of effort to locate me when she learned of my existence. She had learned of my existence when an aunt find some paper work in the closet stating that Mary J. Cromier Saucier verified that she had given her infant son to Amorite and Nellie Johnston and that the child was named Robert Edward Johnston.

I was more than shocked by this news. My mother was dying and my siblings wanted me to visit and speak with her before she died. I couldn't believe what I was hearing: It was too much for me to grasp at that moment.

I thought about it and I made a conscientious decision not to go to the hospital to visit my mother. I still had a lot of pent-up anger and hatred towards her, and I had not forgiven her for abandoning me. I wasn't even sure that I wanted to see her; my emotions were all over the place.

My biological mother died a week later, and my sister called me with the funeral information. She stated that the family wanted me to attend the wake and the funeral. I advised her that I would attend the wake, but that I would not attend the funeral.

The evening of the wake, I got off from work, went home, showered, shaved, and went to the church. I think that I attended her wake more out of curiosity than anything else.

When I walked into the church, I did not know how I was going to react. I slowly made my way down the aisle and approached the casket with an open mind. I just wanted to see who this person was and what she looked like. When I looked down at her, there was a sense of relief; I had no feelings for her at all, neither negative or positive. I felt no love or any emotion towards her.

I spent a couple of hours talking with my siblings after the wake and then returned to my apartment.

The next day, which was the day that my biological mother was buried, I returned to work and I did not even think about her.

I did not attend the funeral, as I had just started a new job and did not want to take the time off. Even though my siblings had put me in the paper and in the obituary as her son, I did not want to deal publicly with the issue at that time. This situation was also very new to me, and I didn't want to be put in a position where I would have to explain anything, as very few people were aware that this white woman was my biological mother.

After my biological mother's death, I was given additional information regarding her by my siblings. None of the information was good. They confirmed some of the information that I already knew. They had learned (mostly through gossip and other information) that I was born at the old Flamingo Hotel in Worcester. My mother had left me at the home of a single woman and never returned for me. I never knew the name of the lady, but she was unable to care for me and she left me at the home of Ethel Mae Grady (Johnson), who cared for me for a year or more. When Miss Grady (Johnson) was no longer able to care for me, I was left with the Helen Richardson family, where I stayed for another year or more. I was then taken in by the Johnston's, who raised me and cared for me until I became a man. My birth was unattended and no record of the birth was ever recorded to their knowledge.

One of my sisters invited me to her home after the funeral because she wanted to get to know me and possibly have a relationship with me. The siblings wanted to get close to me, but I kept my distance. I wasn't ready, prepared, or willing to form a relationship with them at that time. I visited with them on a couple of occasions, but I just did not feel drawn to that situation. For one thing, my siblings were white, and I just did not have any liking for white people at that time.

During one of the visits with my siblings, they talked about our mother and told me what kind of woman she was.

Almost none of the information they gave to me regarding my mother was good. According to my siblings, our mother had five other children. At the time of my birth, she had two children, a boy and a girl, who were placed in a foster home.

My mother and her husband were both alcoholics and were very abusive to each other and the children. The children were placed in foster care due to the abusive and neglectful conditions in the home.

The third child, whom I prefer not to give up too much information on, was also a boy. This child was the product of incest by the stepfather who was married to our mother's mother. My mother's mother, the child's grandmother, took the child and raised him, and he always thought that his mother was his sister.

My mother had conceived this child while she was visiting with her mother who worked as a Chambermaid in a hotel in New York. My mother and her stepfather were inebriated and had intercourse which resulted in her getting pregnant. Her mother felt that she could not send her daughter back to Worcester pregnant therefore she remained in New York until the child was born.

Her mother forbids her husband from returning home and she took the child and raised him as her own.

The boy and his mother, whom he thought was his sister, did not have a good relationship. At some point, while his mother was intoxicated, she made some remarks and statements to the child that allowed him to know the truth about his conception: that his step-grandfather was really his biological father. It is my understanding that he continued to question her about his being her son, but she denied what she had said while intoxicated, even while on her death bed.

They also questioned her about me and the rumors surrounding my birth. Still on her death bed, she denied that I even existed.

I felt that my mother may have denied me in part due to the fact that she was married at the time of my conception and birth to Norman Saucier, and did not wish to acknowledge that she had had an affair with a black man and bring more shame on the family.

According to my sister, our mother and her husband divorced and she later met a very nice man and married him.

She had two children by Mr. DeBigare, a son and a daughter. The daughter was born first and the son was born later. This man required our mother to get her life together and helped her get back the son and daughter who were in foster care, but she never sought to get me back.

I was able to meet the other siblings, with the exception of the one who had died. They wanted to build up a relationship with me but I just couldn't seem to bond with them.

I questioned them about the relationship between my mother and father and they stated that it was an ongoing relationship.

At the time my mother and father met she and her husband Norman were separated and not living together.

They stated that my mother and biological father met at a dance club in Worcester. Their relationship grew out of their love for dancing and they were two of the best dancers in the area.

They were told that my father was a good looking man and was very well off financially. He was also very involved with my mother's entire family and often took food and other things to the house.

I just wanted to be left alone to try to absorb all of this information and try to understand how I really felt deep down in my soul. Having siblings was very difficult for me to grasp; I just was not at peace with my life.

I then started attending church again and joined John Street Baptist Church. John Street Baptist Church was the church my mother helped form and was where I attended church as a child. Pastor Hughes had moved to Worcester from the South and had been the pastor of John Street Baptist Church for a few years at that time.

I enjoyed myself there for a while and did some singing at the church. But after a year there, I found myself losing interest. My personal opinion of the church was that it was for new converts, people who knew very little about the word. The church had a very good beginner's class that was very thorough. The classes helped people to understand salvation, redemption, justification, and the things they needed to know to help them understand their place and position with God and being a new person in the Godly lifestyle. The church was very good and adequate with beginners, but could not move in depth for those wanting to learn more.

My burdens were very heavy and I was not being fed spiritually as I needed at that time. I began to search, going from church to church, crying out for help, but I felt as though no one was listening; not even God.

I started attending another church, located in Shrewsbury, Massachusetts. I don't recall the name of the church, but I stayed there for about a year.

Again, I stopped attending church. While I backslid, I did not deal with people. I would just keep to myself and I didn't enjoy holidays because I was always alone.

The people that I dealt with and all the things that I was involved in were negative. I didn't have any desire to attend church at that time.

This was during the time that I worked as a nursing assistant at the Greenery Extended Care Facility for head injury people. I worked there for a couple of years, and then I went to work for Fed-Ex for about four and a half years.

Being by myself and away from the public gave me the opportunity to get to know myself better. I began to understand myself very well to a greater depth than I had ever done before. This turned out to be a good thing, but at the same time I was in a state of depression.

I had begun to understand this through a Catholic minister who worked at the Greenery Facility. The minister, who was also a counselor, had noticed some things and thought that I appeared to be depressed. We started talking and he began weekly counseling sessions with me.

During the counseling sessions, I learned that the basis for my depression was a result of my abandonment as a child. I had always tried to ignore that because I was taken in and raised by a good family. They raised me well, we went to church, and we went on vacation every year to North Carolina. I never wanted for anything. I always had a place to live, had food on the table, and had both parents in the home. I just focused on that aspect of my life and never knew that I had to deal with the abandonment issue; it had to be put away before I could get on with my life. By dealing with the issue, I eventually came out of the depression and was ready to move on with my life (so I thought).

I left my job with Fed-Ex after about four and a half years because I had no sense of direction and I was having increased difficulty making my scheduled deliveries on time. I had problems finding delivery locations and would get lost easily. The dispatcher would try to give me verbal directions but I was not able to follow them. I have always had a problem with verbal directions; I must be taken physically to the location and shown at least twice how to get there before I am able to go alone; it's just that bad.

I took a job with the Department of Conservation and Recreation in West Boylston and Clinton, Massachusetts, where I worked for four years. My job as a skilled laborer and ranger kept me outside in the woods and walking around the watershed. I already had closeness with nature, but I fully realized how much it meant to me. I just appreciated seeing what God had created, cherished the beauty of it all, and just enjoyed being out in it.

Then one day about nine months later, I decided that I wanted to stop living a negative life style and settle down again.

During the periods when I was heavily involved in church, I was acquainted with a young lady by the name of Mary. I had known Mary for approximately ten years; she was heavily involved in the ministry. She was an Evangelist that had formed her own church and was the pastor. She also appeared to be dedicated and committed with her beliefs. She and her nine-year-old daughter had moved from Worcester back to her home in Atlanta. She stated that she was tired of the stress that came with living in New England.

I had expressed my desire to leave Worcester and start a new life to Mary, and she offered to assist me in getting a job at one of the group homes that she was involved with in Atlanta.

She was already in Atlanta, but was planning to return to Massachusetts to pick up some belongings that she had left with her sister.

This was excellent news for me, and I decided to take her up on the offer, as I saw some potential for a relationship with her.

I really felt torn about leaving Worcester and my friends, but I needed to make a change. I did not want to leave my friend Luther, because we were very close; I tried to talk him into relocating with me, but he stated that he had a family and he could not just pick up and leave. Luther had not forgotten his promise that he would never leave his children or family the way his father had done. I was extremely disappointed but I understood. I felt that I was again losing someone who was very dear to me.

I was able to secure a job at a group home in Atlanta as a residential counselor. The plan was that I would work under Mary's supervision and reside at the group home, and she would help me get acquainted with the city. We would then try to pursue a more personal relationship; I felt that the potential for a good relationship was there.

Mary and I left Worcester in November of 2004 and headed for Atlanta. On the way to Atlanta, Mary and I had several disagreements regarding my driving. I was being extremely cautious and driving at the posted speed limits because I was pulling a trailer and was not familiar with the highways; remember I have no sense of direction. The manner in which I was driving annoyed Mary, and we argued about it for most of the entire trip.

When we arrived in Atlanta, I had already decided that I would not stay, as I had seen personality traits in Mary that I had never seen before, and it allowed me to see that a relationship with her was not possible.

Things had not gone well on the trip down to Atlanta and I was alone in an unfamiliar city with no family or friends. I unloaded Mary's belongings and advised her that I was returning to Worcester. At that point, she became very angry and started cursing at me. She also called me a faggot and tried to attack me physically. I advised her not to put her hands on me, and if she did so, I would call 911.

I did not even stop to rest, as I was totally exhausted by the situation. I left Georgia with my belongings still in the trailer and headed back to Worcester.

On the way back to Worcester, I decided to stop in Gastonia to visit with Ron Dunham, an old friend of mine. Ron and I had previously had a singing ministry together when we both resided in Massachusetts.

I met Ron at an AME Zion Church I attended with my friend Ronald Scott, one of the band members. Ronald Scott wanted to sing a song at the church for his mother's birthday and asked me to help him. We practiced the song a few times and when we went back that Sunday to sing, we realized that Ron Dunham was back in town. Ron Dunham was playing the piano at the church.

After the service the three of us got together and talked. I later went to Ron Dunham's home to visit, and we discussed creating another singing ministry and we did. Ron and I had previously sung together back in the early eighties while he was living in

Worcester. Ron had relocated back to Gastonia around 1982 and stayed there until he returned to Worcester around 2004.

Ron Dunham, Ronald Scott, and I began singing together in area churches. I moved in with Ronald Scott and lived with him until I decided to leave Worcester and relocate in Georgia.

Ron Dunham became very ill and decided to return to his father's home in North Carolina earlier that same year.

When I arrived in North Carolina, Ron Dunham and I decided to form another singing ministry. We sang together at Ron's cousin's church. His cousin was Rev. Thomas Jackson, who pastors his own church and was also a Deputy with the Gaston County Sheriff's Department.

Shortly thereafter Ron became very ill and was hospitalized. Ron passed away early Christmas morning in December 2004. I was devastated when Ron passed. We had had over a twenty-year friendship.

Ron was a very gentle and kind person. I enjoyed working with him musically, because neither one of us would let our egos get in the way. We would always help and direct one another gently in order to sing songs to the best of our abilities. We were not focused on who was the best; we just worked well together and in harmony.

Ron's relatives asked me to sing at his funeral, along with an aunt and Angel, a girl who sang with us in Worcester. Rev. Kirby, the pastor from the AME Zion Church in Worcester, where Ron played the piano, came down to North Carolina to officiate his funeral services. My grief in the loss of Ron was overwhelming. I cried uncontrollably and had to be consoled by my family members. I felt so much pain, and I felt that I wasn't going to recover from this latest loss, but time does help with the healing process.

The night I arrived in Gastonia, I contacted my cousin Janette Meeks, who lived in Kings Mountain. I just wanted to say hello and see how Aunt Janie and the family were doing. I advised Janette that I was just passing through and decided to call to see if I could locate the family. Janette asked if I was staying overnight and I said, "Yes."

She then said, "At least go by the hospital to see Mama," meaning my Aunt Janie. I had not seen Aunt Janie and the family in nearly fifteen years. I was very happy to know that Aunt Janie was still alive.

I went to bed and when I woke up the next morning, there was a religious program on TV. The pastor was preaching on the topic of forgiveness. He stated that forgiveness is good for the forgiver.

The reason I had not been in contact with Aunt Janie and the family for fifteen years was because one of my female cousins had told me that I had never been accepted by the family due to the fact that I was not a blood relative, and that the family never really liked me; they just tolerated me because of Aunt Nellie, my mother.

I was hurt again and the feeling of not belonging anywhere or to anyone gradually started to creep back into my mind. I felt rejected all over again. I believed my cousin and I did not attempt to contact the family or visit with them. I had never attempted to contact the family or question what had been said; I just left and never looked back.

Due to the lack of communication on my part, because they did not know how to get in contact with me, the family and I had not spoken for the past fifteen years.

After listening to the pastor, I realized that the message was directed towards me. I got dressed and went to the hospital to visit with Aunt Janie.

Some of my cousins were there, and they asked me what my plans were; I told them that I was planning to return to Worcester, as I had no other options.

At that point they suggested that I remain in North Carolina but I advised them that I did not have the means to do that. They directed me to another cousin, Paulette Brooks, to see if I could stay with her and Aunt Janie in their extra bedroom until I was able to find a job. Paulette permitted me to stay, and I advised her that I would get a job and be out of her house in a few months.

I immediately put my belongings in storage and started my job search.

It took almost three months for me to get a job. I was finally able to go to work as a Residential Counselor in Gastonia in January 2005. I moved out of my Aunt Janie's home and into my own apartment in Gastonia in March.

Again, I was alone. Even though I had people who considered me to be family and I had met new friends, I still felt that there was a very important part of my life missing.

I went to work in the group home and immediately found the situation in the home to be very difficult to work with. The Program Director at the home had no experience in the field of Group

Home Administration. He was working as a CVS worker when he was hired as the program director due to his computer skills.

Mr. Dean, the House Manager at the group home, also had no experience working in group homes. He was hired solely due to the fact that he had a bachelor's degree. When I and other residential counselors offered ideas to make the situation at the home better, we would be shut down and dismissed by the program director. It was always his way or no way; he really did not know how to run the house efficiently or legally.

It was extremely difficult to perform the job in a positive manner and be of service to the children for their future. The children were simply being housed and no provisions were being made for their future.

At the same time I was working a part-time position at the Gastonia Boys and Girls Club. At the club I met and became very good friends with Mrs. Amelia Massey, George McCaskill (the Director), Jonathan Gordon, Jhonre Smith (a young track star), and a young man we called "House," who was a college student working for the summer.

My job consisted of offering classes to the young boys on how to handle and deal with things such as drugs, hygiene, respect for women, and respect for themselves. We would hold interactive discussions with the children and kept the club stocked. We also went to the movies, on field trips, and to different venues.

CHAPTER 7:
THE BEST THING

My Cousin Lawrence Brooks was given a birthday party at a restaurant in Concord, North Carolina, by his children, and I was invited to attend. At the party I reunited with my Cousin Josie Brooks, who lived in Gastonia. Josie gave me her telephone number and asked me to keep in touch with her. Prior to that evening, Josie and I had not spoken or seen each other in over fifteen years. After that evening, Cousin Josie and I spoke by telephone on a few different occasions, but we did not get together in person.

During one of our telephone conversations I asked Josie if she had any mature saved Christian female friends that she could introduce to me. Cousin Josie said that she would think about it and get back with me, but she didn't. When I asked her again, Cousin Josie stated that she had forgotten, but stated that she would definitely get right on it.

On the next occasion when we spoke, Cousin Josie told me about her friend Elaine, whom she felt would be the perfect lady for me. Cousin Josie stated that her friend Elaine had a heart of gold and was an "Angel on Earth." She also said that Elaine would do anything in the world for people, especially those close to her, whom she loved. She said, "Bobbie, this lady will love you and treat you like a king if you two get together, but whatever you do, do not hurt her."

Cousin Josie only had kind things to say about Elaine, and I told her that I simply had to meet this lady because she appeared to be too good to be real. She stated that she would contact Elaine and get back with me. A few days later, Cousin Josie called me and gave me Elaine's telephone number and stated that it was okay to call her.

On March 29, I contacted Elaine for the first time by telephone. Elaine was a very interesting woman. We just seemed to fit from the start. We talked for hours on the telephone. She asked me to describe myself to her and I said, "I look like an egg with two legs." Elaine laughed and said, "In that case, I know that you are very cute."

Elaine and I set up a date to meet on the following Sunday afternoon, but the date had to be cancelled due to the fact that I was moving into my new apartment. For the next ten days we spoke often by telephone and we grew closer and closer. I felt a great deal of love for her even though I had never seen her.

Elaine was a very busy woman. She was constantly traveling to take care of her business, but she always took time out to communicate with me. Elaine had everything going for herself. She was a mature Christian woman with a beautiful personality, she was so intelligent and a joy to know. Elaine and I made another date to meet on the following Saturday afternoon.

As scheduled, Elaine and I met on Saturday at 4:00 p.m. sharp at Cousin Josie's house. When Elaine walked into the living room, I could not believe my eyes; she was the most beautiful woman, and I just could not even imagine that she would want to be with me. The other amazing thing is that she looked just like my mother, hat and all. You see, my mother was a hat wearer and so was Elaine.

Elaine, Josie, and I spoke for awhile and I asked Elaine if she would like to go out to dinner with me. She accepted my offer, but asked to take a picture with me first. We stepped into Cousin Josie's dining room to take the picture. I was thinking to my-self, "Oh no, another statue picture," when to my surprise, Elaine wrapped her left arm around my waist, placed her face on mine, and said, "Perfect fit." The feeling I had at that moment was over-whelming, I knew then that I truly loved her.

Josie had told me that Elaine was sensitive to cigarette smoke, and since I was a smoker, I asked her to drive her vehicle and I would follow her to the restaurant; I told her that I would explain the reason why later.

We ate dinner at the Golden Corral, and sat and talked for the next five hours. I really wanted to take her home with me but I was to shy to ask. We left the restaurant and just sat in the parking lot in Elaine's vehicle and talked. We finally realized that we had to end the evening, but we spoke again when she arrived back at home.

For the first time in months I was able to get a good night's rest; I slept like a baby. Wow, I was just blown away by this lady; where did she come from? It could have only been a gift from God.

We continued to speak daily for the next week and planned to meet for breakfast on the following Friday morning. Elaine and I met as scheduled at Cousin Josie's house and we rode together to IHOP in her vehicle.

We enjoyed being in one another's company so much. When Elaine dropped me off at Cousin Josie's to pick up my truck, we just sat in the yard, held hands, and talked; I never wanted to let her go.

I immediately called Cousin Josie and thanked her for introducing me to Elaine. Cousin Josie cautioned me again not to ever hurt her. She stated that Elaine had been deeply hurt in the past, and she did not want to see her hurt ever again. I told Cousin Josie that I was very happy and promised her that I would never do anything to mess up the relationship. I told her that this was the best relationship that I had ever had in my entire life.

I felt so much love for Elaine, and I felt that I needed to tell her everything about me and my previous negative life. I confided everything to Elaine; I mean everything. I was surprised when she said that my past was not important, but the future was all that mattered. I was really embarrassed, but I felt that I needed to be up front with her about issues that were very sensitive to me. I said, "Elaine, I need to tell you something that is very important that can really affect our relationship in a negative way."

Elaine said, "Robert, you can always be completely honest with me about everything; I won't judge you."

I then said, "Oh, wow! Elaine, God did not endow me as compared to some other men."

Elaine said, "Robert, sex is not everything and the size of your sexual organs doesn't matter to me; I love you for the Christian man that you are."

I told her that is what all the other women in my life had said, but it was always an issue later. As a matter of fact, the women would call me a faggot. I cried uncontrollably while talking to her, but she was very understanding and supportive. I was really relieved when I had gotten everything out in the open; it felt as though a heavy burden had been lifted off of my shoulders.

Three weeks after we had met face-to-face; Elaine invited me to her house for the first time. As I already suspected, Elaine had a beautiful home, almost as lovely as her.

I was so in love with Elaine, and I could not contain my feelings. I told her that I loved her and she responded, "I love you too, Robert."

The following Saturday, a month and one week after our first face-to-face meeting, at my invitation, Elaine came over to my apartment for the first time. She had prepared lunch for us in a basket, and we had a picnic on the floor in the living room (I had no dining table). I had a small one-bedroom apartment with used furniture but it did not seem to matter to Elaine. We sat on the floor, ate our lunch, talked, laughed, and played like two little kids. I don't think that there was anything that we did not talk about; I was on the top of the world.

Both Elaine and I loved God, music, singing, reading, writing, nature, and many other things. Being with her inspired me to resume writing my poetry. I wrote several new poems because I was so happy.

TEARS OF JOY

WHO SAID A MAN SHOULD NEVER CRY
WAS IT YOU, FOR IT WAS NOT I
WHY CAN'T A MAN WHEN JOY FILLED CRY?
LOOK FROM THE HEART, NOT FROM THE EYE
WHEN LOVE HAS BURNED A PLACE INSIDE
LET TRUE LOVE OUT, LOVE SHOULD NEVER HIDE
DO NOT ASK HOW, TRY TO UNDERSTAND WHY
WHEN A MAN FEELS JOY, A REAL MAN CAN CRY
TRUE LOVE IS NOT A PASSING NOTION
AND IS MUCH MORE THAN JUST EMOTION
THESE TEARS I SHED ARE TEARS OF JOY
SHED BY THIS MAN, NOT BY A BOY
YOU CAN TELL HER JUS HOW YOU FEEL
AND SHE WILL KNOW THESE TEARS ARE REAL
SHE WILL KNOW IT'S LOVE NOT JUST A NOTION
SHE WILL KNOW IT'S MORE THAN JUST EMOTION
WHEN WHAT YOU DO TRULY COINCIDES
WITH THAT LOVE YOU HOLD INSIDE
SHE WILL KNOW IT'S JOY, AND SHE WILL KNOW WHY
IT IS O.K. FOR A REAL MAN TO CRY.
TO CRY TEARS OF JOY

By
Robert C. Johnston   3-6-06

Elaine asked me how I got the nicknames "Beabo" and "Mr. Bob."

I responded, "How did I get the nick names Beabo and Mr. Bob?"

"Well, Beabo came about one evening around 1982 while I was attending a house party in Worcester. A Peabo Bryson record was playing and I began singing over the record as I entered the room. From that point on everyone at the party started calling me Beabo because of my singing. The name just sort of caught on and more people heard it and they also started calling me by that name.

Mr. Bob came about at the different group homes where I worked. It was required by the boy's home, the Boys and Girls Club, and the group homes that the children show respect by calling the adults "Miss," "Mrs.," "Mr.," or "Sir." The children started calling me "Mr. Bob" because it was easier to say than "Mr. Robert."

After finishing our picnic, Elaine and I enjoyed talking, listening to music, and watching sports on the television. Elaine was lying on the living room floor; I think that she was asleep and I was sitting in my favorite chair. I looked down at her lying there and she was so beautiful, like an angel; I loved her so much and wanted her so badly. I don't really know what happened to me, or how it happened, but the next thing I knew I was on the floor beside her and we were embraced in a kiss. We made love, and it frightened me tremendously after I realized what we had done. I immediately stood up and left the room because I didn't know how to handle the situation.

Elaine also appeared to be in shock and she asked me, "Robert, what is the matter? Don't just walk away; we have to talk about this."

I didn't know what to say or how to react. I was shocked at what I had done and that she had responded to me; I was just plain frightened. It was like being in a dream; I couldn't believe that it was real.

Elaine and I spent several hours talking about what had happened between us, and it was so late at night that I asked her to stay over. We spent that night together just embracing one another and I knew then that I wanted to marry her and spend the rest of our lives together.

Both Elaine and I were concerned about having sexual relationships before marriage, and we talked about it and agreed that we must abstain until after we were married. We knew that this would not be easy because we were so deeply in love.

Elaine and I continued to date; I finally officially asked her to marry me in June, and she said yes. I wanted to get married right away, but Elaine wanted to wait until she wrapped up some of her business and I was more financially stable.

We planned our wedding and set the date for the following year on April 29, 2006.

I was on top of the world and I knew that God had performed a miracle in my life. It was to be a new beginning with someone who truly loved me for who I was and could accept all of my faults and short-comings. Elaine and I celebrated every day; she was so kind and loving.

The following Saturday we attended my cousin Jennifer's wedding, where I sang a solo. Elaine was the most beautiful woman there; she was captivating. A gentleman even came over and asked to take a picture of her. It made me feel like a giant when she asked me to sit next to her for the picture. I was so very proud to be the man in her life.

In the next weeks, Elaine and I came up with a plan to help me get out of debt and get me back on my feet financially. She was willing to help me get a loan to consolidate all of my credit card debt and assist me in getting a car that was more economical than the Chevy Blazer truck that I was driving. My truck was not fuel-efficient, and I was spending over half of my weekly income on gas to get to and from work.

She also offered to let me move into her son's vacant house until our wedding in order to save on rent. I could live rent free if I agreed to keep up the property and grounds. I would repay the loan at a rate of $300 monthly. My monthly truck payment alone was well over $300 at that time.

At the same time Elaine's house was undergoing extensive renovations. There was a lot of equipment on the site that made it difficult to get in and out of the property. We discussed it and decided that she needed to move temporarily until the renovations were completed. The agreement was that we would move together to her son's house; we would have our separate bed and bathrooms, but would share the kitchen and other spaces.

I offered to give Elaine one half of the rent that I would be saving, but she advised me to keep it so that I would have a nest egg for myself when we got married. I wanted to be able to give her a nice engagement ring, but she said that that did not matter to her. She stated that she had more rings than she could ever possibly wear, and if I insisted upon giving her an engagement ring, I could purchase one from her collection at a minimal cost.

Elaine and I had planed to announce our engagement and marriage plans at our Christmas party in December.

Before finally moving from my apartment in Gastonia, I would sometimes spend the weekend in Elaine's guest quarters just to be near her. I recall one night we were lying in bed talking. Elaine and I were making plans for our wedding, and she was so excited about helping me. I couldn't believe what was happening; I started to cry uncontrollably. Elaine just embraced me and asked me not to cry and stated that everything would be all right.

I just shook and cried out, "God is restoring me," and I truly believed it at that moment. We made a solemn promise to each other that we would always love one another and that we would not betray each other's trust. This was to be our best and last relationship; we were going to be together for the rest of our lives. We made so many promises that night, and our future together was sealed.

For the next two months, I was the happiest man on the planet. I was working at the group home while looking for a better job and Elaine was busy trying to help me in every possible way. She was also trying to get my true identity established and establish a record of my birth.

I gave her all of the information that I had found in my parents' paperwork after their death. There were several letters in the paperwork from an attorney in Worcester, indicating that my parents were attempting to adopt me legally for several years but had never completed the process.

The first letter was received from Campbell, Lewis & Smith, Attorneys at Law, dated October 26, 1956. The letter reads:

CAMPBELL, LEWIS & SMITH
ATTORNEYS AT LAW

KLEBER A. CAMPBELL, JR.
BURTON A. LEWIS
JAMES M. SMITH

EVANGELINE V. TALLMAN

October 26, 1956

521 STATE MUTUAL BLDG.
340 MAIN STREET
WORCESTER 8, MASS.

TELEPHONE PL 6-4609

Mrs. Mary Saucier

Dear Mrs. Saucier,

Mr. and Mrs. Johnston have asked me to help them in adopting your son. I think it would be a wonderful thing because it would give him a good home and would also complete their home since they have no other children.

I understand that you are willing to consent to the adoption but that you want to avoid being involved any more than necessary. I shall respect your wishes but it is very important that I have a chance to meet you and talk with you if I am going to be successful in getting the adoption through. It would save me a lot of time and would be a great favor to me if you would be willing to talk with me in my office with my promise that you would not be embarrassed in any way and that your visit would be just between the two of us.

Will you please call me on the telephone and then we can make some arrangement that will be okay for both of us. I will be at my home in Grafton from seven o'clock on tomorrow evening (Saturday) and also Sunday morning until ten o'clock, and Sunday evening from seven o'clock on. My number is Vernon 9-4713 and I hope very much that I will hear from you.

I know you are doing what is best for your boy and I would like to be helpful in any way possible to accomplish this adoption because I believe the Johnstons are very fine people and love him sincerely.

Sincerely yours,

KAC/lb

The second letter from the law firm was dated April 2, 1957. The letter reads:

CAMPBELL, LEWIS & SMITH
ATTORNEYS AT LAW

KLEBER A. CAMPBELL, JR.
BURTON A. LEWIS
JAMES M. SMITH

EVANGELINE V. TALLMAN

831 STATE MUTUAL BLDG.
340 MAIN STREET
WORCESTER 8, MASS.

TELEPHONE PL 6-4609

April 2, 1957.

Mr. and Mrs. Amorite W. Johnston,
53 Clayton St.,
Worcester, Mass.

Dear Mr. and Mrs. Johnston:

I am very glad to tell you that the contact which I have been trying to make has worked out successfully twice and that I have been able to sit down with the person concerned in Judge Wahlstrom's office to discuss her part of the problem. I am about to leave on a business trip for about ten days, but soon after my return would like to see you. I think we can really get rolling now.

Cordially,

Kleber A. Campbell, Jr.

The third letter from the law firm was dated March 20, 1961. The letter reads:

CAMPBELL & SMITH
ATTORNEYS AT LAW

KLEBER A. CAMPBELL, JR.
JAMES M. SMITH
EVANGELINE V. TALLMAN
JOHN M. STELLATO

March 20, 1961

SUITE 512
340 MAIN STREET
WORCESTER 8, MASS.
TELEPHONE PL 6-4808

      This is to certify that the records in my office show that Robert Edward Johnston (sometimes known as Harold Saucier) was born on June 22, 1951, and is accordingly nine (9) years old.

      Sincerely,

The fourth and final letter from the law firm was dated September 20, 1973. The letter reads:

CAMPBELL & SMITH
ATTORNEYS AT LAW

KLEBER A. CAMPBELL, JR.
JAMES M. SMITH

SUITE 625
340 MAIN STREET
WORCESTER, MASS. 01608
TELEPHONE 756-4608
AREA CODE 617

September 20, 1973

Mr. and Mrs. Amorite W. Johnston
34 Providence Street
Worcester, Massachusetts

Dear Mr. and Mrs. Johnston:

Enclosed is the adoption petition about which I talked to Mrs. Johnston over the telephone. Will each of you please sign the first and second pages where your initials appear in pencil and then have Robert sign the bottom line of the first page where his initials appear. If you will then return this form to me and also give me the year in which Mr. Amorite Johnson was born, so that I can complete the form I will file it in the Probate Court.

Sincerely yours,

KLEBER A. CAMPBELL, JR.

KAC/tw
Enclosure

SUITE 625
340 MAIN STREET
WORCESTER, MASSACHUSETTS 01608

Mr. and Mrs. Amorite W. Johnston
34 Providence Street
Worcester, Massachusetts

The search for my birth record would take over a year to complete.

The process was initiated by contacting Mrs. Pauline McNulty at the Massachusetts Registry of Vital Records and Statistics. We explained what we knew to Mrs. McNulty and we were advised to request a Negative Statement of Birth for Robert Edward Johnston. A search for the birth record would then be completed. The search resulted in no record being found.

Our next contact was with the Massachusetts City Clerk, Mr. David Rushford. We repeated the known facts surrounding my birth and requested his assistance in getting a birth record established. We were asked to provide the following information in order to conduct the search.

1. A certified copy of my biological mother's marriage license

2. Proof of residence for my biological parents, which could be obtained from a census report, voter registration card, a utility bill, etc.

3. A copy of the Negative Statement of Birth

4. A request for change of name

The Commonwealth of Massachusetts

City Of Worcester
Office of the City Clerk

359687

Copy Of Record Of Marriage

Registered #: **222**

Place of Marriage:	WORCESTER, MA
Date of Marriage:	FEBRUARY 6, 1942
Name of Groom:	NORMAN T. SAUCIER
Surname After Marriage:	SAUCIER
Residence:	WORCESTER, MA
Birth Date/Age:	22
Marriage Number:	FIRST
Occupation:	UNITED STATES ARMY
Birth Place:	GARDNER, MA
Name of Father:	THEODORE J. SAUCIER
Maiden Name of Mother:	IRENE M. DAME
Name of Bride:	MARY J. CORMIER
Surname After Marriage:	SAUCIER
Residence:	WORCESTER, MA
Birth Date/Age:	16
Marriage Number:	FIRST
Occupation:	AT HOME
Birth Place:	WORCESTER, MA
Name of Father:	PHILIP CORMIER
Maiden Name of Mother:	LUCY A. BURKE
Married By:	MALCOLM C. MIDGLEY, JUSTICE OF THE PEACE AND CITY CLERK
Residence:	WORCESTER, MA
Date of Record:	FEBRUARY 7, 1942

I, the undersigned, hereby certify that I am the Clerk of the City of Worcester;
that as such I have custody of the records of marriages required by law to be kept at my office;
I do hereby certify that the above is a true copy from said records.

WITNESS my hand and the SEAL OF THE CITY OF WORCESTER at Worcester on
June 28, 2005.

David J. Rusoford
City Clerk

Sent: Thursday, July 07, 2005 3:52 PM
Subject: e-mail request

> Dear Mr. Johnston, Your parents were listed in the 1951 Worcester City Directory,
> one of our primary sources to locate persons living in Worcester. There name
> appeared on pg. 932. Good luck with your search.
> WPL REF Staff-----------------------------------
> Reference Department
> Worcester Public Library
> 3 Salem Square
> Worcester, MA 01608
> (508) 799-1655
>
>

Reference Department
Worcester Public Library
3 Salem Square
Worcester, MA 01608
(508) 799-1655

Sareault Sylvain (Vera I) mach opr Hobbs Mfg Co
Sarette Arth (Mary) trainee b 5 Clifton
—Mary R Mrs clk N Co r 752 Pleasant
—Paul (Mary) clk h 752 Pleasant
—Rudolph T (Beatrice) elec truck opr Rockwood Sprinkler Co h 9 Albert
Sargeant Gladys Mrs hsekpr r 37 Monadnock rd
—Martha r 25 Roxbury
—Mary E wid Chas r 20 Converse
—Ruth I studt Belmont tlosp r 107 June
Sargent Bertha r 161½ Austin
—Beverly A clk Woolworth's r 455 Park av
—Blanche wid Chas R h 130 Lincoln
—David L (Marjorie C) slsmn Westinghouse Elec Corp h 69 Randall
—Ella A r 47 Townsend
—Eliz M wid Henry r 39 Beaver
—Ernest A b 554 Pleasant
—Ernest A (Rhea) tool mkr H&R Arms Co h Auburn
—Esther wid Reed W r 125 Lamartine
—Exterminating Co (Wm H Sargent) 3 Hudson
—Frances slsmn Waite Hardware Co r 18 Bourne
—Francis A (Cath J) comp Commonwealth Press h 455 Park av
—Francis G jr, misc wkr Worc Lithograph Corp r Leicester
—Guy hlpr Wyman-Gordon Co r Auburn
—Harold E (Frances E) wtchmn Telechron Inc h 17 Watson av
—Harold R (Maria E) mech 601st Signal Light Construction Co. MNG
—Harry A time study eng N Co r Holden
—Harvey E chauf J B Garland & Son Inc r Northboro
—Herbert E ofc mgr Kalamazoo Sales & Service Co h 5 Wellesley av
—Kathleen L Mrs tel opr NET&T Co r 7 Fairbanks
—Laura A r 7 Norwood
—Leon A (Mary E) asst formn Parker Mfg Co h 47 Townsend
—Lorraine Mrs clk F W Woolworth Co h 3 Hudson
—Marion E Mrs waitress Central Kitchen h 1 West
—Mary r 718 Main
—Priscilla clk N Co r Leicester
—Rachel L Mrs clk Mass Protective Assn r 21 Freeland
—Ralph (Kathleen D) insp Wyman-Gordon Co h 7 Fairbanks
—Reed W jr, wire drawer Thompson Wire Co h Shrewsbury
—Richd M (Lillian M) slsmn h 343 Burncoat
—Robt J v-pres Hard Chrome Die Inc r Shrewsbury
—Robt G (Julia C) (F H Germain & Co) elec wkr h 39 Beaver
—Robt Z jr (Virginia M) sla eng F H Germain & Co h 37 Amherst
—Walter H treas Acme Realty Co and used furn 312 Pleasant r 563 Main
—Wm H (Mary J) (Sargent Exterminating Co) h 3 Hudson
—Wm H jr (Lorraine E) television h 305 Mill
Sargentelli Amelia Mrs h 68 Suffolk
—Eliza wid Elldamo h 94 Hamilton
—Jeannette M box mkr Whitcomb Envelope Co r 68 Suffolk
—John P (Mollie E) chauf United Wholesale Grocery Co h 97 Cutler
—Louis (Tillie) glass ctr h 1½ Carroll
—Michl F (Linnie D) chauf h 15 Wall
—Romeo (Rose) receiver General Automotive Supply Co r 94 Hamilton
Sargento Rosanna r Home Farm
Sargiumas Wm B pntr Brewer & Co Inc r Shrewsbury
Sarian Arth (Anita) tester Johnson Steel & Wire Co Inc h 22 Ekman
Sarison Nettie hsekpr r 559 Park av
Sarja Andrew (Helen A) opr Henry L Hanson Co h 105 Gage
—Annie W mach hlpr Worc Taper Pin Co r 26 Belmont
—Arne C classifier N Co r 28 Belmont
—Arth r 28 Belmont
—Klaus (Sandra) h 28 Belmont
—Loretta press opr Killeen Mach Tool Co Inc h 18 Cottage
Sarkala Adolph h 7 Bliss
Sarke — tchr WPI r 34 Dean
Sarkees Yazbeck T instr WPI r 49 Institute rd
Sarkis Adele wid Peter r 45 Prospect
—John pdlr r 29½ Prospect
—Jos h 29½ Prospect
—Margt T sewer Sol & S Marcus Co r 29½ Prospect
Sarkisian Andrew (Mary) shoe wkr h 29 Green Hill av
—Arakel (Arnoush) died Sept 15, 1950
—Armen (Marie) (Sarkisian's Service Station) r 38 Uxbridge
—Haigh R (Eliz) chauf Ry Exp h 146 Beverly rd
—Harry r 2 Glenwood
—Hovannes died Sept 29, 1950
—Kasper wire wkr Thompson Wire Co r Auburn
—Lucille asmblr Worc Taper Pin Co r 2 Glenwood
—Mary Mrs h 88 Summer
—Nishan h 724 Main
—Nishan K (Youghaper) lab Fremont Casting Co h 69 June
—Onush wid Arakel h 2 Glenwood
—Sultan wid Eleazar H h 38 Uxbridge
—Vartan r 15 Florence
—Wm (Michelina) window installer r 21 Hill
Sarkisian's Service Station (Armen Sarkisian) gas sta 205 Shrewsbury
Sarli Angela M clk r 9 Merrifield
—Baptiste (Maria) lab h 9 Merrifield
—Battista sweeper N Co r 9 Merrifield

SARLI
—Vito J r 26 Institute rd
—Vito J studt WPI r 9 Merrifield
Sarnlad Eric E (Alice) N Co h 7 Birchhill rd
—Tage W (Alice Y) wheel sharer N Co h 17 Fulton
—Thos N (Nora M) mach opr The Vellumold Co h 43 King Philip rd
Sarosick Stanley J steel wkr h 51 Orchard
Sarra Michl (Mary) lab h 18 Hill
Sarrete Gabriel (Helen) chauf Logan Div US Env Co h 21 Cutler
Sarsfield Dennis W (Ida M) brkmn N Co
—Ida Mrs h 60 Plantation
—Patk K h 26 Almont av
Sartwell Allen r 4 Langdon
Sarty Alva nurse Odd Fellows Home r 40 Randolph
—Anson slsmn Table Talk Pastry Co Inc r 66 Chandler
—Beatrice M ofc sec Mirick, O'Connell & DeMallie r 12 Denny
—Bernice M wid Wm C h 12 Denny
—Doris R ofc sec Standard Service Bureau r 12 Denny
—Ella N Mrs lodging house 77 Chatham h do
—Harriet E sten r 77 Chatham
—Hazel P clk Carleton Engraving Co r 12 Denny
—Helena W Mrs sec Mass Protective Assn r 103 Mower
—Jas E (Maude C) h 52 Woodland
—Lester Heath (Helena W) senior clv eng County Eng h 103 Mower
—Max A (Jeannette E) formn Jas P Brown h 1 Bliss
—Melvin (Doris) chauf h 1 Redding et
—Milton J (Emily F) dairymn h 35 King
—Ray baker r 66 Chandler
—Wm R mach Heald's Mach r 12 Denny
—Willis E (Elva) furnished rooms 242 Franklin h do
Sarvala Eliz wid Emil h 69 Laurel
Sasek Donald A studt r 26 Institute rd
Saska Andrea clk Livingston Photo Service r 4 Milton
Sasse Ernest H stick grinder N Co r Holden
—Marilyn A clk Mass Protective Assn Inc r Holden
Sasserville Leo A appr Progressive Tool & Die Co Inc r Spencer
Sasseville Albert heat treater Mass Steel Treating Corp r Spencer
—Robt floor mn Thompson Wire Co r Spencer
Sasso Vincent (Angela) genl contr 13 Locust av h do
Satter Nathan (Marion M) mgr M & M Transportation Co
Satterberg Milton G J (Rachel E) pastor Harlem St Baptist Church h 26 Forsberg
Satti Victor F mach Christie & Thomson Inc r Dudley
Saucier Albert (Anna L) hlpr h 25 Locust av
—Albert H wire wkr G F Wright Steel & Wire Co h 25 Locust av
—Anna L Mrs nurse r 25 Locust av
—Armand E (Ann T) shoe laster h 3 Allen
—Constance N sten W H Hill Envelope Co r 117 Highland
—David H wire drawer Worc Wire Works r Spencer
—Dora B wid R Eug A h 6 Wall
—Emery E (Eva N) chef Boynton Cafe h 117 Highland
—Eulalie Mrs r 541 Grafton
—Eva Mrs smstrs Allen's r 117 Highland
—Geo L bar tndr Boynton Cafe r 117 Highland
—Grace P studt nurse Hahnemann Hosp r Webster
—Irene baker Worcester Club r 217 Russell
—Leo J (Meena) serv mn h 110 Perry av
—Mary J waitress J J Newberry Co r 27 Fox
—Norman T pntr r 217 Russell
—Omer G greaser The Henley-Kimball Co r Spencer
—Robt (Muriel) hlpr h 20 Mendon
—Robt E (Muriel) insp r 12 Arthur
—Roland G (Antoinette E) meat ctr Mrs Mary E Iandoli h 12 Arthur
—Theo J (Irene M) supt h 217 Russell
Sauers Grace L Mrs sec r 26 Dustin
—Harry L (Grace L) nurse h 26 Dustin
Saulenas Anna Mrs gill box opr M J Whittall Associates r 50 Lafayette
—Frank V (Mary M) electn h 16 Grammont rd
—Jacob wire wkr Johnson Steel & Wire Co Inc h 131 Mechanic
—John chauf r 50 Lafayette
—Jos T (Jessie A) chauf h 50 Lafayette
—Julius (Elinor) chauf h 2 Colton
Saulnier Adelard plater Worcester Brass & Electro Plating Co r 11 Davis
—Albert r 23 Institute rd
—Alda r 86 Arthur
—Alf (Bernice) h 11 Davis
—Chas A furnished rooms 133 Main h do
—Claremont, USN r 51 Suffolk
—Gertrude M counsellor Family Service Organization r 6 Bowdoin
—Henry J (Ruth M) pkr Whitcomb Envelope Co h 110 Pilgrim av
—Jos A wire wkr G F Wright Steel & Wire Co h 86 Arthur
—Josephine B stitcher Teekla Garment Co r 86 Arthur
—Leo J (Margt R) chauf h 36 Norfolk
—Lucy M lndrs City Hosp r 86 Arthur
—Mary press opr Culver-Stearns Mfg Co r 87 Norfolk
—Nolin wid John J h 51 Suffolk
—Omer J (Mary) chauf h 87 Norfolk
—Ora opr Baldwin-Duckworth r Dodge

FORM R-580

G 60790

REGISTRY OF VITAL RECORDS
AND STATISTICS

The Commonwealth of Massachusetts

STATE DEPARTMENT OF PUBLIC HEALTH

Date *April 22, 2005*

This is to Certify that a search has been made of the records in this office for the

~~birth~~
~~marriage~~ of *Robert Edward Johnston*
~~death~~

Throughout the records of the Commonwealth for the years: *1946 – 1955*

and that said record has *not* been found. For further search you are respectfully referred to the clerk of the city or town where the event occurred.

Stanley E. Nyecry

Registrar of Vital Records and Statistics

FORM R-568

G 64023

REGISTRY OF VITAL RECORDS
AND STATISTICS

The Commonwealth of Massachusetts

STATE DEPARTMENT OF PUBLIC HEALTH

Date *May 31, 2006*

This is to Certify that a search has been made of the records in this office for the

~~birth~~
~~marriage~~ of *Harold Theodore Saucier*
~~death~~

Throughout the records of the Commonwealth for the years: *1951 – 1960*

and that said record has *not* been found. For further search you are respectfully referred to the clerk of the city or town where the event occurred.

Stanley E. Nyecry

Registrar of Vital Records and Statistics

Over the next few months, Elaine contacted funeral homes, utility companies, the public library, cemeteries, and any other agency that she felt might be able to help in our search.

We were able to locate a record of my biological mother's death in June 2005 and were able to secure enough information to finally obtain a copy of her Record of Marriage.

My biological mother, Mary J. Cormier, was married at the age of sixteen to Norman T. Saucier; age twenty-two, in Worcester, Massachusetts, on February 6, 1942, by Malcolm C. Midgley, Justice of the Peace and City Clerk.

Mary J. Cormier's occupation was listed as at home. Her birthplace was Worcester, and her parents were Philip Cormier and Lucy A. (Burke) Cormier.

Norman Saucier's occupation was listed as United States Army. His birthplace was Gardner, Massachusetts, and his parents were Theodore J. Saucier and Irene M. (Dame) Saucier.

The copy of the obituary obtained from Callahan Brothers Funeral Directors read as follows:

> Mary J. (Cormier DeBigare)—75
> July 21, 2000
> Worcester:

Mary J. (Cormier) DeBigare, 75, of 39 Westminster Street died Friday July 21, 2000 in Memorial Hospital after an illness.

She leaves three sons, Richard McKenna, Robert Johnston and Brian DeBigare, all of Worcester, two daughters Diane Fulton and Jean Nowalski, both of Worcester, 14 grandchildren and 12 great grandchildren. Another son, Norman Saucier, died in 1997.

Born in Worcester, she was the daughter of Philip Cormier and Lucy (Burke) McKenna and lived here all her life. Mrs. DeBigare attended Sacred Heart Academy. She worked for the former OK Wool Company of Worcester and Parker Metals, retiring many years ago.

The funeral will be Tuesday July 25 from Callahan Brothers Funeral Home, 61 Myrtle St., with a Mass at 10 a.m. in St. Paul's Cathedral; 15 Chatham St. Burial will be in St. John's Cemetery, Worcester. Calling hours are Monday July 24 from 5 to 8 p.m. at the funeral home.

The Worcester Public Library was able to provide proof of residency for my biological mother and her husband by the 1951 Worcester City Directory. Their names, address, and occupation appeared on page 932 of the directory.

Mary J. Saucier was listed as a waitress and her address was at Newberry Co.

Norman Saucier was listed as a painter and his address was at 217 Russell.

Elaine and I started attending church together. We visited several different churches, trying to find one that would fulfill our needs. We wanted to make God the first priority in our lives and wanted to make sure that we were in a church that would feed us spiritually.

In order to supplement my income, I decided to purchase disc jockey equipment and book engagements for weddings, church functions, parties, reunions, and other social events. The flyers read:

"LET B.J. THE SINGING D.J.
Make a Joyful Noise for You (Psalm 66:1)
At Your
WEDDING – CHURCH FUNCTIONS
PARTIES – REUNIONS
AND OTHER SOCIAL EVENTS
(B.J.) Bob Johnston
704-718-3348"

This was my first experience at disc jockeying and I had a lot to learn. I was able to secure a few jobs, but there was no great demand for my services; I'm sure that this was due partially to the fact that I was new in town and was not well known.

I quickly learned that disc jockeying was not an easy job. I had to spend several hours preparing for the events by attending rehearsals and meetings; the business was not very profitable either, but I continued to work at it.

Elaine and I attended the Roberts' Moore, and Brooks 100th. Year Family Reunion in August and we had a wonderful time. I met several family members that I had never met before including Congressman Mel Watts.

Again Elaine had to leave town on personal business and I missed her very much.

While Elaine was away something happened to me; I can't explain it, but I gradually started having doubts about the relationship, and I got worried that it would not last. All of my old fears started creeping back into my mind. I started questioning myself and Elaine's love for me.

I couldn't understand why such a beautiful, successful woman who had every thing going for her could love a pathetic nobody like me. After all, I had nothing to offer her, not even a decent job. The feelings of worthlessness continued to grow, and the more Elaine showed her love and tried to help me, the worse I felt. I felt as though I was losing my mind, and I was fighting for my sanity; I had to be dreaming. Elaine could not possibly love me, and I decided that I had to run before I got hurt and dumped again; I knew in my heart that I could not survive another let down.

I started to imagine negative things about Elaine, and I invented things to make myself hate her. I would say to myself, "She is just like my mother; she doesn't love me and she will eventually leave me." I finally convinced myself that I had to leave her before she left me. I also started to resent her success and wanted what she had; I became very jealous and envious of her.

The last week in September, Elaine returned home and we went car shopping. We traded my Chevrolet Blazer truck in on a Toyota Camry, which I would use to get to work and transport us to church on Sundays. I was happy about the car, but I was sad that I could not be the man in the relationship.

Over the next week, I gave my situation a lot of thought, and I concluded on my own that I could no longer continue in the relationship with Elaine. I did not feel worthy and I felt less than a man. I could not take care of myself; how could I take care of a wife? I agonized over my decision to break off my engagement to Elaine because I knew how badly it would hurt her, but I felt that I would hurt her even more if I married her. I could no longer play the game and make excuses for my actions; I wasn't worthy of her.

On Tuesday morning, October 4, Elaine made breakfast for us, and while sitting at the table eating, I told her that I could no longer continue with the relationship. Elaine tried to embrace me, but I physically pushed her away and said, "You are always here."

I could see that Elaine was in shock; she left the table and went into the bathroom and sat on the garden tub, sobbing. I just stood there not knowing what to do or what to say. Elaine asked what was wrong, and I just said, "I can't do it anymore." Elaine tried to talk with me, but I had nothing to say; she finally gave up and left.

A few days later I signed a promissory note to repay the money that was owed on the loan for the car and consolidation of my credit cards.

I continued to live at Elaine's son's property, but I did not want to have a relationship with her. I don't know what really happened to me; I just saw my mother in Elaine, and I could not handle my emotions. Elaine not only looked like my mother, but she had her exact personality. She was a beautiful, strong black woman who always dressed well and wore hats just like my mother. She worked constantly in the church and always tried to help people, just like my mother.

All of the anger and unforgiveness that I felt for my mother was now being directed towards Elaine; I actually felt hatred towards her. I didn't want to have her near me at all; she was now just another person that I could use to get what I wanted.

Elaine never stopped being a friend to me. She invited me to dinner for Thanksgiving and acted as though nothing had happened. I really could not understand why she continued to be kind to me after the way I betrayed and disappointed her.

At Christmas she gave me a ring, scarf, and a gift card as Christmas presents. I asked her what the ring was for; I was thinking in my mind that it was an engagement ring. She replied, "It's just a gift; I thought that the color green would look good on you. Don't worry, there's no hidden agenda; it's only a gift."

She just continued to treat me with kindness and love.

The following January, Elaine's son sold the property where I was living, and I had to move into her guest quarters. She wrote this letter to me:

Tuesday, January 24, 2006

Dear Robert,
    WELCOME TO YOUR NEW HOME!!!
    I would like to thank you for taking your time out last night to talk with me and answer some of the questions which I had. I truly appreciate it.
    I feel so much Joy this morning because a very heavy burden has been lifted from my Heart ("And ye shall know the truth and the truth shall make you free").
    When I stated to you last night that I loved you more than myself, I did not mean it in the way you understood it. I meant that I was totally committed to you and devoted to our life together. When you hurt, I hurt twice as much, when you cried, I cried even harder, when you were going through difficult times on the job and in your personal life, I felt all of your pain and I prayed harder, when you were in need, I tried to provide what was needed. I trusted you with my heart and my life; that's what true love and commitment is.
    I feel a true sense of broken trust, but I cannot dwell in that place as I am so marvelously blessed by God. God placed an enormous amount of love and compassion for others in my heart and soul and he rewards me abundantly every time I give.
    Even though you don't love me, I will continue to love you as God has commanded.
    The reason I say that you don't love me is because of the way you left me and the way you have treated me since. You don't seem to care about how this ordeal has affected me and my life, how I feel, or what condition you have left me in. You were my life and I could never have imagined that the Robert I fell in love with could be so cold and cruel and lacking in compassion? Even though you hurt me deeply, I loved and cared enough for you to want to make sure that you would be okay, even if the relationship did not work out.

Your refusal to talk with me really cut deep, because that was the one thing that we could always do and I counted on it. But instead you kept things hidden and just turned your back on me and walked away without any discussion or an honest explanation.

I realize now that I really never had a chance with you because you were not looking for a wife or commitment when we met. I don't regret meeting you, but I feel that the timing was not right. You were going through so much turmoil and changes in your life and I don't feel that you have resolved a lot of those issues. I too was not in a settled situation, but I was always completely honest with you and I changed my whole life to be with you.

Any way, as my grandmother always said. "That's water under the bridge" and "Don't cry over spilled milk, you can't pick it up."

From the very beginning of our relationship you had me under a Microscope, dissecting me, my every move, and my words, looking for flaws in my character. I, on the other hand, was looking at all of the beautiful and wonderful qualities that you had to offer and accepted you as you were, both good and bad. You have said many things that have cut me deeply, but I realized that you are human. I thought that you were truly in love with me and I did not take these things to heart; I understand, support, etc. Have you ever thought about what you took from the relationship?

It did not matter how much I loved you or what good I did for you. You can only remember what you say was a cutting remark from a fallible human being. If the relationship had been remotely important to you, you would have discussed the remark with me when it happened and we would have worked it out.

I feel that you were simply caught up in the moment when we first met and when you realized how serious I was about our getting married, it frightened you to death and you looked deep for an excuse to end the relationship and I guess you found one or two. It amazes me that you don't acknowledge or say anything about the fact that you knew that I loved you with all my heart, was fully committed to you and our life together, would have never done anything to intentionally hurt you, had the highest respect and regard for the person that you are, and would have done anything in the world for you; I guess that part of me was insignificant to you and carried no weight in your heart or conscience.

Your unforgiving spirit concerns me because you have placed yourself above God. Remember you once said that "God forgives what man will not." God forgave you, but you can't forgive me for whatever I might have said because you don't want to.

Don't get me wrong, I feel no anger and the hurt is getting easier to deal with. I don't want to revisit this subject because I have stayed in this place long enough. It's time to move on.

I am writing my book and it is going to be a best seller; made for the movies.

I pray every day for your happiness and success. I love to hear you laugh as that is what I want for you: JOY!

Thanks again,

Be Blessed.

Elaine

I was even more upset with Elaine when I read her letter. I didn't like anything that she had to say. I knew that she had been hurt deeply; I just wanted her to get on with her life.

I had moved on with my life and I was not looking back, no matter what. I have never been able to have a fulfilling and satisfying relationship with a woman. The relationships were always good in the beginning but would always end badly. I don't know if I have ever given any relationship a fair chance because of my fear of rejection.

Even after all of these years, I just could not seem to forgive my mother for not legally adopting me. I felt that a lot of my problems would have been resolved if I had been legally adopted.

Not only did I feel unwanted but I also did not feel worthy as a man. I didn't have a decent job and could barely take care of myself. I was living on Elaine's property and I could not even afford to pay her rent. I had agreed to keep up her lawn and grounds but I just did not seem to have the strength to even do that.

I knew that I was in a state of depression but I didn't have anyone to turn to or anyplace to go. I just felt so completely alone even though I was being shown love on a daily basis. Elaine would always cook and make sure that I had something to eat every day.

She never tried to be cruel to me; I still could not seem to accept her for the kind and generous woman that she was. She never tried to do anything to hurt me but I still saw her as one of my enemies. I even grew to hate her more and more, and I didn't understand why.

Elaine appeared to be such a happy person, living in her own little world with nothing to worry about, and I resented the fact that she had everything going for her and I had nothing. She had such a beautiful home, a nice car, property, and money. She could buy anything that she wanted at any time, and I couldn't even afford to buy her an ice cream cone.

I was really feeling sorry for myself, and I decided that it was best that I just give up on having a relationship with women. I came into this world alone, and I have been alone all of my life, and I guess I will die alone.

Elaine would not give up on me. She kept trying to talk with me and wanted us to try again to build a new relationship, but I was still resisting her. I guess you could say that I felt that I had a sense of power over this situation, and I wasn't budging.

I stopped by Elaine's after work one afternoon and she invited me to sit down because she wanted to talk to me. She had a lot of questions for me and just wanted me to be open and honest with her as a friend; she wanted to bring some closure to what happened in our relationship. We talked for hours but I still could not open up and be completely honest with her, even though she gave me every opportunity to do so.

The next day Elaine gave me another letter that she had written after our conversation. I knew that she was trying to get through to me but I was just determined to stand my ground no matter what. I was the man now; I was in control of this situation and that made me feel good.

The letter read as follows:

Friday, February 10, 2006

Dear Robert,

I stayed awake until 2:00 a.m. this morning thinking solely with my head about our conversation yesterday. Even though you don't think so, I have really been listening and paying attention to everything that you have said and watching your actions over the past five months and I have come to the following conclusions.

I am not angry or upset with you and I don't want to get back together with you because I don't want to be with a man who is not committed and truly in love with me. But it is important for me to let you know what I think and how I feel about you.

First, I feel that you are full of games and lies. I also feel that you are very evil spirited, insecure, and don't know what it is to be a true friend.

Secondly, you profess to be something that you are not, and you truly believe that you are right and have all of the answers.

When we first met, I thought that you were the answer to my prayers and I thought that you were the most sincere and completely open and honest Christian man that I had ever met in my entire life.

After all of the turmoil and drama that you say you have experienced with women in the past, I believed that you and I as promised would always be completely open and honest with each other about our feelings. I thought that we were bonded like Super Glue and could overcome any and all obstacles, but I was wrong.

*Judging from what you have said, you knew very early in our relationship that you had issues with me and my being a strong black woman with a beautiful mind, but you just held it inside. You too are **very controlling** and are not willing to bend* *to fit in order to have a mature relationship with any woman and you are not willing to give any woman a fair chance. When you truly love a person, you are always willing to try even if it does not work out. A committed Christian man would have at least sat his partner down and discussed the issues and stated that he could not continue in the relationship if changes were not possible. You keep saying that you would not ask me or any other woman to change, but you do so with your actions. You assumed that I would not be happy if I was not in control and nothing can be further from the truth, but you were not willing to deal with the issue and find out for sure because you did not want to be in the relationship at all. The truth is, you had already made up your mind to leave the relationship and no amount of discussion or reasoning was going to change your mind. The sad thing is that you feel that it is ok for you to be controlling and bull headed, but no one else had that right. My mistake is that I thought that I was helping you because you kept saying that you did not know these things and I would have to tell you. How was I to know what you knew and what you did not know? If helping you was offensive, then I am very sorry.*

I really don't want to be in control of anything in the future, and I won't be. I have changed my lifestyle completely, and my total focus is on my Lord and Savior. I just want to serve and praise God for the rest of my life.

I really feel sad for you because you are missing a lot of your blessings by being so stubborn. Do you really want a Zombie as a partner? I want an intelligent and loving man at my side who will know what to do in any circumstance or emergency, not just a yes person.

When you asked me to marry you, you did not mean it and you were not committed to a life with me, period! You needed an excuse, and you found one that was convenient, and that is the reason why you weren't willing to try to work out the issues. You were afraid of the results.

You kept saying that you didn't have anything to bring into the relationship and you were absolutely right. All I wanted was your love and you proved over and over, time and time again, that you didn't have love for me.

I just wished that you had handled ending the relationship with more compassion and in a different way; after all I am a human being with a heart. If you wanted out of the relationship, all you had to do was to say so in a truthful and loving way.

You keep saying that I am a good person, but you treated me as though I was nothing. Even when I was in the hospital, you told me the story about your friend's wife pretending to be sick to get sympathy; how cruel. You know that I have heart problems and high blood pressure, but you could have cared less if I lived or died and that is why I would never call you when I didn't feel well.

You continued to make cutting remark after remark and I ignored it because I knew that you were upset and hurting and I loved you enough to understand.

You seem to have a lot of resentment and jealousy towards me and I don't understand it. I have always had your best interest at heart and as you know was willing to do anything for you.

I also want to make it clear to you that I made love to you because I trusted you and I thought that you were sincere about marriage. If you recall, and you recall everything, after the first time, I stated that we did not have to make love again until after the marriage. You were the one who said, "Oh no, it's too late, we've already tasted the fruit." I have asked God to forgive me for that sin and he has. When I make love again it will be with my husband.

You have told me to move on with my life, and I am attempting to do so, but you keep making remarks that are *hurtful to me. I am not hard core as you are and it takes time for me to get over someone I truly love.*

How could you ask me if it is ok for you to bring another woman into my domain? How would you feel if I bought another man into your domain? Please do not disrespect me in that way. Since you plan to move in September, perhaps you can visit her at her home or take her to a hotel if necessary.

You stated that you would like to be friends, but I don't think so. Your definition of friendship is not the same as mine. I tried to be a friend, but you continually turned me down cold. You can't even attend church with me; how can you be a friend? My friends are very loving towards me, and they do not have a problem with my character. We love each other for the wonderful people that we are, and we can always forgive, because we know that no one is perfect. We cherish our friendship and would do anything in the world to help each other. We know that no matter what, we have a shoulder to lean on in a crisis. Even when we withdraw, we can always count on each other.

Your definition of friendship appears to be: it's ok if you are there for me, but to hell with you.

I pray daily for you and your happiness and I hope that your life will be filled with true love and joy. I am not an evil woman and I wish that you had been able to see the loving kind person that I am and not focus on the materials.

By the way, I have never heard you say that you are sorry for hurting me or anything. That says a lot to me.

Be Blessed.

Elaine

By February I had gotten totally frustrated with my situation and was planning to return to Worcester; I contacted Elaine to advise her of my plans. Elaine became very upset and said, "No, you can't be serious. You love North Carolina, and I know that you love the fact that you can attend so many different churches." She also stated that if I go, she would go with me and I told her that that was not possible.

Elaine then searched the Internet for job vacancies and she located a vacancy for a custodial position at Springfield Elementary School in Stanley, North Carolina. She contacted me to see if I was interested in that position. I told her that I was, and she faxed my resume to the school.

I was contacted by the school and an interview was scheduled. Mrs. Whitlock, the principal, interviewed me and I was offered the job the next day.

I was feeling really good about this job and was again looking forward to a good future. The pay was not that much but I would have benefits and medical insurance.

I thanked Elaine for her help and again advised her to move on with her life. I told her that she needed to get out sometimes so that she could meet someone. She could not meet anyone by sitting in the house all of the time. Elaine wrote me another letter.

Monday, March 6, 2006

Dear Robert,

I want to thank you for the advice that you gave me yesterday and I plan to take it. You are right, I have always put everyone else and their needs before my own, and that was wrong. I am very concerned about the welfare of the people that I love and cherish, but I must now take care of myself and my needs first.

I have decided to sell everything that I own here as soon as possible and get on with my life in another country. Life is so precious and none of us have any time to waste.

Though it truly hurts to do this, I must let you know that you will need to find another place to live in the next thirty days, as this property will be rented out next month. I was planning to wait until September because I was concerned about you and wanted to help, but as you said, you don't need a mother.

I also thought about just selling this house, but I feel that I must respect my grandmother's wishes, as she loved me with all of her heart, and I promised her that I would keep the property in the family. I don't know if I will ever live here again, but maybe my grandchildren will enjoy it. Just thinking about the plans that I had for a life here with you makes me feel very sad, but life goes on and I must go with it.

I would appreciate it if you would return my post office box key so that I might close the account.

I picked up some telephone books for you to check for apartments. If you would like for me to make some calls for you, please let me know.

I would like to make arrangements with you to deposit your monthly loan payment in my account each month. If this is not possible, please let me know and I will make other arrangements.

I wish you all of the best that life has to offer for your future. Call me if you have any questions.

God Bless You.

Elaine

I called Elaine when I received her letter. I knew that it would be impossible for me to find a place to live within the next thirty days. I was still not financially stable and had no savings to fall back on. I had been trying to find a room to rent and had mentioned my situation to all of my friends and family but no one had offered to help me.

My pride has always gotten in the way of my using good judgment and making sound decisions. I didn't want to ask Elaine for any more help, as I was already feeling less than a man where she was concerned. Even though she knew my situation and did not appear to let it affect her caring for me, I just could not show her my true feelings.

I needed Elaine's help but I was too proud to let her know how desperate my situation was. I was accustomed to being in charge of most situations in my life, whether good or bad. Elaine did not owe me anything, especially after the way I had treated her. She was really a stranger to me, and I had not taken the time to really get to know her. My focus was always on what she had as opposed to what I had (which was nothing). My resentment of her and her status in life outweighed my ability to reason in a mature manner.

I also continued to see her as a mother figure instead of the friend that she was trying to be. I was so totally focused on not giving her any false hope for a future with me that I overlooked the friendship that she had always shown towards me.

After thinking about my financial situation and talking with friends and family, I decided to ask Elaine for an extension of time. I left a message on her answering machine explaining what I needed and advised her that I would move out as soon as possible.

The next day after getting my message, Elaine sent me a written response to my request. I always got very upset when I received a letter from her because it was usually something that I really did not want to hear. In fact, it would just make me dislike her even more. I guess I just really could not accept the truth and really didn't want to hear it, especially from her.

March 7, 2006

Dear Robert,

I got your message this morning when I returned home and I really don't know what to say. I am so confused about what you really want. You tell me to get on with my life and I am finally taking your advice, but now you want me to wait. I think that I have waited long enough for someone who is a stranger to me and doesn't care about me one way or the other; I am just a means to an end.

I have tried being a friend to you since you decided to walk out on our relationship, but you didn't want that, and continually pushed me away. When I invited you to dinner or asked you to do things with me, even go to church, I was not trying to get you in bed or have sex with me. You still don't get it; I can't make love to a man who says he doesn't love me. Sex is not everything and I only made love to you before because I thought that you were sincere about our getting married and I loved you with all of my heart. I still love you, but in a different way.

I was simply trying to be what I thought we both needed: A FRIEND. A person who would always be there through thick and thin, who would love unconditionally, even as a friend, one who knew your heart and appreciated you for the person that you are, who had experienced a lot of pain in their life and knew how to care, who remembered the long trusting conversations that we had and would not repeat the same mistakes. I wanted and needed you to be my "BUDDY," that's all.

I don't think that I will ever be able to trust another male, because I haven't met one in my entire life that is trustworthy and that is sad. If you recall, I had issues with males before I met you and I told you about some of my experiences and hoped that you were different. But unfortunately, you have hurt me more than anyone else in the past and I have done more to help you than anyone else in a very short period of time, because I thought that you were trustworthy.

Have you ever taken a minute to really think about how you have treated me and how you broke my heart? Even if it means nothing to you, have you ever imagined the pain I feel and how betrayed and hurt I am?

You said that you didn't ask me to help you and you are right, but what you don't say is that I helped you solely because you and I were getting married and were going to be together forever. So I was helping us, not just you. Do you really think that I would have invested so much money in a person who was lying to me if I didn't trust you 100%? I trusted you with my life and you betrayed me.

I am in North Carolina now because of you. You wanted to live in the country and I wanted you to be happy. I would have never spent all of the money to renovate the house if I knew that you had any doubts. I just wished that you had thought enough of me to tell me about your doubts before it was too late.

You were always suspicious of me and my motives because you knew that you had not done the right thing by me. You cannot say that I have ever done anything to hurt you.

But on the other hand, I have been deeply hurt by you and you don't appear to care, not even as a friend. I was always there for you when you were hurting and going through hell on your job; you could depend on me no matter what. But I on the other hand had to depend on my other friends to be there for me when you walked away without an honest explanation or any support.

You said that you don't give people a second chance, but the truth is you don't give yourself a second chance. You have made bad choices all of your life which has left you in a very bad position. You are in a "Strong Hold Pattern" and you have not realized how you are letting it destroy your life. You need to shake it off and get real with yourself. You are a grown man *and you need to really take a good look at your actions and the choices that you make. You can't change the past, but you can start making the choices now to change your future.*

Life is very precious and we are living in the last days. All I want is PEACE and LOVE in my life. I know that God will bless me with the desires of my heart and I will be happy.

You have moved on with your life and you have a new lady in your life and I wish you the best. I hope that you will be completely honest with her and not hurt her as you have hurt me.

I won't know for sure what date next month the renter will need the property. I will meet with them next week to discuss this and I will let you know.

Be Blessed.

Elaine

CHAPTER 8:
No Break

I started my job as a custodian/grounds keeper at Springfield Elementary School in Stanley in January 2006. I really liked the job and enjoyed the people that I worked with. I also had the opportunity to mentor some of the young children, and I enjoyed that very much. The children all called me "Mr. Bob" and so did the staff members.

I had worked less than two months at Springfield Elementary when I became very ill. I had been experiencing chest pain and discomfort for over a week. Elaine and her friends were on a vacation trip at Lake Lure and I had no one to call on. At the same time my Cousin Andre was admitted to Carolinas Medical Center in Charlotte with a collapsed lung. I went to Charlotte to visit with Andre, and I had so much chest pain and found it hard to breathe. I was sweating and felt very weak, but it never occurred to me that I was having problems with my heart.

Elaine returned home on Sunday and I briefly spoke to her on my way out to visit with Andre. I did not mention to her the fact that I felt ill. The following morning I left for work and I was feeling so bad that I called Elaine and told her what was happening.

Elaine told me to stop wherever I was and she would come to pick me up and take me to the hospital. I told her that it was okay and that I was going by the school and let them know that I needed to go to the hospital to be checked out.

When I arrived at the school, I could hardly stand up, and I almost passed out when I leaned over to pick up a rock that was in the driveway. I told the principal that I needed to go to the hospital, and she refused to let me drive. She had the secretary call 911 and I was rushed by ambulance to Gaston Memorial Hospital. Blood tests were done in the Emergency Room, and the results indicated that I had had one or more minor heart attacks.

I called Elaine to let her know what was going on and asked her to pick up my car at the school. Elaine stated that she would and that she would stop by the hospital to see me and bring me some clothing and personal items.

I was admitted to the hospital and immediately placed on blood-thinning medication. After speaking with the cardiologist, I was advised that a heart catheterization would be performed the following morning.

Elaine arrived at the hospital as promised later that afternoon and stayed with me until I forced her to leave. She would not leave until I called my family to let them know that I was in the hospital.

I had not informed my family because they had enough to worry about with Andre being in the hospital. Elaine advised me that I should call my family as they had the right to know that I was in the hospital, and that they would be very hurt to learn it from someone outside the family. She reminded me that this was my family and that they loved me very much and that it would not be right to keep my illness from them. I took Elaine's advice and called my family and before I knew it, my hospital room was full of family members.

Elaine was satisfied and agreed to leave, but stated that she would be back early in the morning and would be with me after the heart catheterization was completed.

The heart catheterization was performed early Tuesday, March 14, and it revealed that I had a ninety-five percent blockage in my heart artery. The doctors also noticed that I was having problems with my breathing and referred me to the Sleep Center. The doctors placed a stent in my artery to open it up.

I was then taken to the Recovery Room, where Elaine was already waiting.

Barbara, the secretary at the school, and my cousin Doris came in later to check on my condition.

Later that afternoon, I was taken to my room in the Coronary Care Unit. My supervisor, Jason, and other staff members stopped by the hospital to visit.

The following morning I was discharged from the hospital. Elaine picked me up and took me home. She ran errands and cooked for me as she normally had.

I was placed on medical leave for seven weeks and I followed up at the Sleep Center, where I was diagnosed with sleep apnea. I was advised to use a sleeping machine to regulate my breathing to help prevent additional problems with my heart.

One day after my surgery I was thinking about my heart condition and I was having a difficult time believing that I had actually had one or more heart attacks. Then I recalled an incident which took place one night on my job at the group home.

I was having severe chest pain and I thought that I was suffering from indigestion. I called Elaine and described the pain that I was having to her and she advised me to call 911 immediately and have them transport me to the hospital. I told her that I would be okay and that I could not leave the boys because regulations required that two workers be on the premises at all times to supervise the boys.

Elaine asked me, "Do you have any aspirin or is there some at the house?" I told her that I did not know. She then asked me where the other worker was and I told her that he was on the telephone trying to contact the supervisor.

Elaine asked me for the address where I was working and stated that she would come over and stay with the boys until the supervisor could be reached and a relief worker sent. I explained to her that she could not be there because she was not authorized to be on the premises.

Elaine advised me to ask my co-worker to locate the aspirin and insisted that I take at least eight tablets. I followed her instructions and took the eight aspirin and I felt much better. I then said to her, "Elaine, I hope that you are not making me over dose on all of that aspirin." Elaine insisted that I go to the emergency room and I told her that I would in order to get her to stop talking.

When I got off from work about two hours later I went home and directly to bed.

I did not realize it at the time, but God and taking the aspirin saved my life that night.

The episode inspired me to write another poem called "Second Chance." I knew that God had given me a second chance by sparing my life, and I was truly grateful.

I had not forgotten that Elaine had given me a thirty-day notice to move over a month ago and I sent her the following note:

4-9-06

Elaine

I just want you to know that I am still trying to find a living situation. Knowing you want me out of here makes it uncomfortable and I am honestly trying—even to rent a room from someone. I just haven't found anything as of yet.

Robert

Elaine and I talked and she agreed to give me a five month extension until September 1 due to my medical condition.

While I was recovering from my surgery Elaine surprised me with a fifty-fifth birthday party. She had me convinced that I was the DJ for a special occasion one of her friends was having for her mother's eighty-fifth birthday. She had her friend call me and discuss the arrangements and my fee. It didn't even occur to me that the party was being planned for me. I had never had anyone do anything like that for me since my parents died. I was told that Calvin Edwards, International Jazz Artist, would also be performing that evening. This really made me feel a little nervous because I didn't know how I was going to measure up to an international performer.

Elaine also asked my cousins Janette and Andre to help out at the party. Janette was to help with the serving and Andre was to park cars.

On the Saturday afternoon of the party, I was getting my equipment set up when the international jazz artist and the videographer arrived. There were lots of activities going on that day, and it was all very exciting. The caterer and several helpers also arrived to set up the food tables.

Elaine came into the party hall and asked everyone to step out so that the ladies could change into their uniforms. I stepped outside with Andre and he tried to get me to go inside of the house. I wanted to stay outside and watch the guest as they arrived.

It was a very hot afternoon and Elaine came out and ordered us to get out of the sun. She said, "Either go into the house or into my office; it is too hot to be standing outside." Andre and I went into her office and sat down to talk. About thirty minutes later Elaine came in and asked us to come to the party hall to help her out.

Man! Was I surprised when Elaine opened the door and everyone screamed out, "Happy Birthday, Robert" and started singing "Happy Birthday" to me? Man! What a shock to learn that it was actually a surprise party for me. My Aunt Janie, my cousins, Gaston County Commissioner Pearl Burris Floyd, and some of Elaine's relatives were there. I was so shocked that I didn't know how to respond. I just put my head down on the table and tried to breathe in some air.

Elaine gave me a birthday card with an I-O-U for one Delayed Record of Birth. She stated that Attorney Thomas W. Bodkin, Jr. in Worcester was working on getting the birth record, but it could not be sent before the party.

I couldn't believe that my Aunt Janie and cousins had kept this secret from me; especially Andre.

There was a money tree, an over-the-hill gift basket, a walking cane with a horn, mirror, medicine container, and other things, a wheelchair, portable potty, balloons, and several other gifts for me.

A moving speech and tribute about me and my life was given by Aunt Janie. Gaston County Commissioner Pearl Burris Floyd also spoke kind words of congratulations to me even though she did not know me personally. Man, what a surprise! This was the first surprise birthday party that I had ever had in my life.

Elaine had asked me to record some of my gospel tracks to be sold at the party, but I learned that she had purchased the tracks and placed them in a gift basket and had given one to every guest.

I just could not believe what was happening, and I really didn't know how to act. Instead of being happy, I was frightened and I just wanted to run away and hide. I kept leaving the party hall to go outside in order to get some fresh air and to think.

I finally realized that I hadn't even thanked Elaine for all that she had done for me. I went over to her and embraced her and said, "Thank you." She said, "You are very welcome."

She then advised me that the money tree was one of my gifts and that I should remove the money, as the DJ advised her that two people had removed some of the money from the tree. I went over to the tree with Elaine and we counted out close to $500. I was still in such a daze that I just couldn't get excited.

Two weeks later Elaine presented me with a letter that contained the Delayed Record of Birth for Harold Felix Saucier, which had been recorded at the City Clerk's Office in Worcester on March 5, 1974.

448019

THE COMMONWEALTH OF MASSACHUSETTS
CITY OF WORCESTER
OFFICE OF THE CITY CLERK

COPY OF DELAYED RECORD OF BIRTH

REGISTERED NUMBER: 6006

CHILD

Name: HAROLD   FELIX   SAUCIER
Date of BIRTH: JUNE 22, 1951
Sex: MALE
Place of Birth: WORCESTER, MA

MOTHER

Name: MARY   J   SAUCIER
Maiden surname: CORMIER   Age at last birthday: 26
Birthplace: WORCESTER, MA
Residence: WORCESTER, MA

FATHER

Name: NORMAN   T   SAUCIER
Birthplace: FITCHBURG, MA
Age at last birthday: 31

Date of RECORD: MARCH 5, 1974

I, the undersigned, hereby certify that I am the City Clerk
of the City of Worcester; that as such I have custody of
the records of births required by law to be kept in my
office; I do hereby certify that the above is a true copy
from said records.

Witness my hand and the SEAL OF THE CITY OF WORCESTER
at Worcester on this 11th day of July 2006.

DAVID J. RUSHFORD
CITY CLERK

I didn't know the circumstances surrounding how this record was produced. The only thing I can recall is that I went to the Clerk's Office in 1974 to request a way that I could get a potential identification card and the City Clerk asked me to give him two weeks to check the records for any possible information.

When I returned in two weeks, I was told by the City Clerk that he was unable to find any records relating to my birth. I was never shown or given any information, and I do not know how the record was produced. I had no knowledge of its existence until I received it from Elaine as a birthday gift.

Elaine's thought was that the Delayed Birth Record was produced by my biological mother during the process to get me legally adopted by the Johnston's.

July 18, 2006

Dear Robert,

Enclosed is a copy of your Delayed Birth Record, which I promised you (Happy Birthday!). The next step is for you to request a legal change of name. Attorney Jeannette Reeves at 1219 Fallston Road, Shelby, North Carolina is willing to assist you. If you wish, you may call her to discuss the filing fee for the paperwork. The telephone number is 704-487-1234.

I wish you the very best of everything in the future and hope that this will help you to bring some closure to issues which are preventing you from living a joyous and fulfilled life.

Last week you implied that you wanted to stay here until January but unfortunately I won't be able to accommodate you beyond your previously requested extension date of September 1.

I have put my life on hold and sacrificed enough for a person who is a stranger to me, a person who is uncomfortable around me, who does not appreciate me, and who does not care about me or my well being.

I don't understand why you feel that it is ok to say that you don't want to have a life with me because you don't have anything to offer me, but you are perfectly willing to accept what I have to offer you as a person. It doesn't make sense. That just says to me that it is ok to use me, but not ok to be with me.

Life is too short and too precious and I do not have any more time to waste. I cannot walk backward into the future.

You are right; we do have major character differences. You are a taker and I am a giver. The fact is that I was always willing to share what I have with you even if you didn't love me; that's just the person that I am. I say what I mean, and I mean what I say; I can't say the same for you. I have love and compassion for others. You have love and compassion for Robert.

My heart is aching and I am so tired of getting my feelings hurt by you. I have never tried to intentionally hurt you or make you feel bad, but you seem to get some sort of pleasure out of hurting me and it is time for it to stop. I have enough things upsetting me and I don't need the added pressure.

You say that you are a friend, but you don't know how to be a true friend. You continue to treat me like the stranger that you are. You may think that it is cute to call me ma'am, and set on the opposite side of the room when I try to talk with you, and act as though I have the plague. It hurts me deeply and I don't deserve the disrespect and pain. You have made it painfully clear that you have no love or regards for me and I accept that, because I realize that you are not my friend and have never really cared for me.

My true friends talk to me with respect; they enjoy being around me, they laugh and joke with me, we share what we have, no matter how large or small, we don't care about things, we care about the heart, we accept each other for who we are; we celebrate the differences, and embrace each other when we are in pain. There is something about a touch; it has a healing effect. A touch means so much, even from a stranger when you are going through. Your response to my pain is to stand on the opposite side of the room and look at me as though I was an alien. I feel that I am just that revolting to you, that you can't even bear being near me. Can you even imagine how you make me feel?

I don't recall making any advances to you that would lead you to believe that I am trying to seduce you. I am past that stage of the relationship, as a matter of fact, I don't even like your new personality and actions. I feel that you are self-absorbed and have no regards for anyone except Robert. No matter what type of relationship it is, marriage, friendship, or other, there must be mutual understanding, respect, and caring. Relationships don't just happen by chance; they must first be desired, worked on, prayed over, and forged on the hard anvils of conflict resolution, truth telling, and sacrificial love.

You are like some of my family members. You don't see the goodness in my heart; you only see the material things around me and you can't get past that. You can't separate the business from the personal. My heart means nothing to you. You don't even realize that I am a human being with human feelings. I never looked at what you had; I only looked at you and your love for God. Nothing else mattered. You permitted your pride and ego to destroy what could have been a beautiful and loving relationship. Material things fade away, but true love last forever.

It reminds me of something that I once read that was observed by C. S. Lewis: "To love at all is to be vulnerable. Love anything, and your heart will certainly be wrung and possibly be broken. If you want to make sure of keeping it intact, you must give your heart to no one, not even to an animal. Wrap it carefully round with hobbies and little luxuries; avoid all entanglements; lock it up safe in the casket or coffin of your selfishness. But in that casket—safe, dark, motionless, airless—it will change. It will not be broken; it will become unbreakable, impenetrable, and irredeemable. The only place outside Heaven where you can be perfectly safe from all the dangers of love is Hell." This reminds me of you.

I have done everything possible to show you how much I care for you as a human being and a friend, but you are not receptive at all. I never lied to you, I never cheated on you, and I always held you in the highest esteem. I was so proud of you and you made my heart dance and my smile as bright as a shining star. I thought that you were the greatest, and I loved you with all of my heart and only wanted the best of everything for you. But, I realize that the relationship has always been one sided and frankly I am tired of it. I am tired of being called ma'am and being treated as though I do not exist. I just want peace and joy in my life and I can't have it as long as you are here. I deserve to be loved, respected, and cared for as much as you and everyone else.

I also realize and accept the fact that you never really loved me. You want me to believe that you did, but you lied to God, to me, and to yourself. You love Robert and Robert alone. When we met you were going through a very traumatic period in your life and you needed someone to lean on and I was that person.

Have you forgotten how we used to talk hours on end, how we confided in each other, how we couldn't seem to get enough of each other, and how we trusted each other? I haven't forgotten, because it meant so much to me to finally (I thought) have a man who appreciated the love that I had to offer and wanted to share his life with me.

When I sit on the front porch on Sunday afternoons, I always remember how you said we would spend our Sunday afternoons together studying the word of God and building memories. I would have never changed your life and hurt you the way that you have hurt me.

But, as soon as things got better for you, I was no longer needed and you didn't hesitate to can me. The relationship meant so little to you that you didn't even want to try to talk or work out the differences, whatever they were; only God and you know for sure.

I don't know the new person that has emerged and I don't like him at all, but I will always love the Robert that loved me. I do believe that you are capable of loving another person, but I realize that, that person is not me; never has been, and never will be.

You treated me as though I was nothing but garbage; you had no mercy or compassion for me and never considered the hurt and pain that I felt.

I gave up so much for you, but it doesn't matter; I was doing what I thought was making you happy and you did what made you happy. It didn't matter how it affected Elaine or her future. Just remember, you reap what you sow.

I would like to remind you of what true love is:

"Though I speak with the tongues of men and of angels, and have not love, I am become as sounding brass, or a tinkling cymbal. And though I have the gift of prophecy, and understand all mysteries, and all knowledge; and though I have all faith, so that I could remove a mountain, and have not love, I am nothing."

(I was sure that you and I had the love of God and what it took to have a committed and loving relationship. I thought that our love was so strong that **nothing** *could remove it; how wrong I was. Perhaps I am just an unrealistic dreamer, but I know that God said that the greatest gift of all is love and his word does not lie.)*

"And though I bestow all my goods to feed the poor, and though I give my body to be burned, and have not love, it profiteth me nothing."

(I always give all that I can with love and I expect nothing in return.)

"Love suffereth long, and is kind;"

(You suffered less than six months, and I continue to suffer, but that means nothing to you as you are ok. I have always been kind to you and have been a true friend. You are a very cold-hearted person; nothing seems to touch your heart. You don't appear to cherish true love or human feelings.)

"Love vaunteth not itself, is not puffed up;"

(You are a very vain person and you have an ego that is out of this world. You are very materialistic and appreciate things more than the heart or goodness of a person. Things are all vanity; nothing belongs to us, it all belongs to God. He is letting us use it temporarily while we are here on this earth. He gave it to us to share and to be a blessing to others. You have not yet realized that pride comes before the fall.

It hurts when you make fun of me when I make a mistake; I never even call it to your attention when you make a mistake because we are all fallible human beings.

Even though I don't always agree with what you have to say, I always listen to you and hear you out, but you on the other hand will get puffed up and walk away if you don't like what is being said.)

"Doth not behave itself unseemly, seeketh not her own, is not easily provoke, thinketh no evil;"

(You are selfish and self-centered; only you and your feelings matter. There was nothing that you could have asked for or needed that I was not willing to give, but I asked you for one thing, voice lessons, and you couldn't even do that. You did say that you didn't ask me for anything, but you were fully aware of why I was doing what I was doing. Your reasoning was immature and childish. A moral person would have said, "No, I can't accept your help because I am not sure that the relationship is going to work out." What type of person will ask a woman to marry him, make a commitment, accept what she has to offer him, and then walk away less than two weeks later without an honest explanation or discussion of the issues? We have major character differences or I don't give myself a second chance is behaving unseemly. Do you not think that your actions are pure evil? If you do not think so, then please tell me what they are. God created us all uniquely different for a reason and he forgives us 777 times a day and you can't overlook some character differences or forgive at all. This means that you have not fully matured as a Christian.)

"Rejoiceth not in iniquity, but rejoiceth in the truth;"

(I am an honest person and I am not a proud person. I will tell you the truth even if it hurts, but I can't get you to be completely honest with me about anything.)

"Beareth all things, believeth all things, endureth all things;"

(You can't even bear being near me. You don't believe in the power of God and of prayer or is it that you didn't believe in the relationship? You hope for very little, but God placed you on the front porch of opportunity and you didn't even have to knock, the door was opened for you and my hands were stretched out and you said, "No thank you, God, I don't want or need it." You turned and walked away. You have not endured anything that has to do with my well-being.)

"Love never faileth; but whether there be prophecies, they shall fail; whether there be tongues, they shall cease; whether there be knowledge, it shall vanish away.

"For we know in part. ..."

"But when that which is perfect is come, then that which is in part shall be done away."

(Nothing is more important than the love and nurturing of another human being; everything else will fade away.)

"When I was a child, I spake as a child, I understood as a child, I thought as a child; but when I became a man, I put away childish things."

(You have not fully matured as a man or a true child of God. You are still walking in darkness. You cannot be honest with me or yourself. Yes, the truth hurts, but you owe me the truth, not a pack of lies that make you feel better. I am mature enough to accept the truth, but are you mature enough to be completely honest?)

"For now we see through a glass, darkly; but then face to face; now I know in part; but then shall I know even as also I am known.

"And now abideth faith, hope, love, these three; but the greatest of these is LOVE."

I will always cherish the good memories and love that I have for the very special and caring man that I met on March 29, 2005.

It is time for me to move on mentally and for you to move on physically. Seeing you every day does not make it easy for me and I hope that you understand that it is not my wish to make your life difficult. You ended the relationship almost a year ago and you should have been prepared to leave at that time, it was your decision; I had no input into it and it is not fair to me for you to continue to be physically present in my life accepting my kindness when you have no regards for me or my feelings.

I feel that you have taken my kindness for weakness, but maybe one day you will understand what I have on the inside that makes me love unconditionally.

If we as Christians cannot be obedient to God's word here on earth and let go of the past, then how do we expect to get into Heaven?

There are a lot of people in this world who are truly hurting and starving for love and affection, and I feel that it is past time for me to redirect my attention to where it is needed and appreciated.

I would appreciate it if you would call me Elaine and not ma'am or miss.

I didn't say all of this for you to be concerned about my friendship towards you because I am a true friend and I will never change. I just need to let you know how I feel. I have vented and I know that it doesn't matter to you, but I feel better. Thank you.

Your friend in Christ,
Elaine

P. S. Please forgive any grammar or spelling errors. I'm not perfect.

I moved from Elaine's property in the middle of September. I really had no place to go and I did not have the money to afford an apartment. I initially moved in with my Cousin Andre in his apartment in Charlotte, but I could not stay long because his lease forbids people who were not on the lease from moving in.

I had contacted a friend of mine who lived in California and had made arrangements for her to move out to North Carolina and share an apartment with me in Gastonia. I was sure that our arrangement would work out, so I went into further debt to secure a two-bedroom apartment and to purchase new furniture.

My friend came to North Carolina, but things did not work out between us, so she returned to her home. I was then stuck with a one-year lease that I could not afford and an additional mountain of debt. At that point I had no choice except to give up the apartment and move back to Massachusetts.

I moved back to Worcester in January of 2007. The stories that I told Elaine were that I was going to stay with a friend, Jamie Skitters, until I got settled again; that was not the truth.

Jamie was a younger kid in the neighborhood when we were growing up. He was a few years younger than me and this made a big difference when we were growing up, and we never hung out together as children.

Jamie's father was in the military and Jamie was a "Military Brat." Jamie was also a collector of albums and had an extensive collection. Initially we started talking about music and then Jamie started talking about church and at that point I directed him to Grace Community Church of God.

Even though I was no longer in attendance at the church, I still felt that it was a good place to be as their teachings were good. Jamie eventually started attending the church.

The second reason that I gave her was that my move was precipitated by my grandson's aunt needing assistance in raising him. My daughter Nicole was currently serving time in prison in Framingham. After her release from Framingham, she may have to serve time in Connecticut for criminal convictions in that state. My grandson is currently in the custody of the Commonwealth of Massachusetts.

I told Elaine that I recognized that I had always been a very selfish person in my life, and I felt that it was time for me to give back. The opportunity to help my grandson arose, and I thought that this would be a good time to start giving back. I thought that if I could make a difference in the life of this young man, it would be worth the sacrifice that I would have to make.

If I could keep him out of jail and help him to avoid some of the pitfalls that I had faced, it would be good.

Who was I fooling? I was lying to myself; the truth was I had to make a move due to my financial situation. My pride, as usual, kept me from admitting the truth and asking for help. I felt really foolish; I just did not know how to handle this situation.

I returned to Worcester and nothing went right for me. I thought that I would be able to get a job immediately, but that just did not happen. I ran into one obstacle after another. I was miserable and I felt like kicking my own behind for moving back to Massachusetts.

I looked daily for a job for the first three months and every road led to a dead-end. I applied for a job driving a school bus, but I had to take additional tests to get the required endorsements for Massachusetts. The endorsements that I received in North Carolina were not sufficient for the Commonwealth of Massachusetts.

I was assured that I would get the job, but it would initially be on a substitute basis until an opening becomes available. Even after getting hired, I would not be eligible for any benefits until after one year.

It was an ordeal that I had not counted on and I was ready to return to North Carolina, but my finances wouldn't permit me to do so until September.

At that point I had no alternative, except to ask for help. I had no resources to purchase my medications, which I needed to sustain my life. I didn't even know how I was going to apply for help either, since I had no birth record in my name.

I am blessed in the fact that Elaine continued to send me some of my needed medications each month. Elaine has proven to be a genuine friend and I love her for that.

To make matters worse, I have started smoking pot again to relieve some of the stress and pressure. I became very weak and needed an escape from my problems temporarily, but I only made my situation worse.

I was living with a friend and her two children, who did not want me there. It was a constant battle there with the children, and I didn't feel like a man because I was unable to contribute to the household.

Even though I was born and raised in Worcester, I no longer felt that it was my home. I have friends that I no longer feel comfortable associating with. I have really made a mess of my life and I don't see any end to it.

My drug and alcohol use steadily increased, and I didn't know what to do to turn the situation around. I felt as though I was in a storm and I couldn't get out of it. I have made so many mistakes in my life, and my judgment has really been lacking.

Things became so unbearable with my life and living arrangements that I decided to take a big chance and ask Elaine for her help to get out of here before it was too late. I called Elaine and left her a message asking if she had gotten married and asked her to call me back.

I was not available when Elaine called back but she left a message stating that she was not married.

I wanted to return to North Carolina and start my life all over again. I prayed that Elaine still had enough love in her heart for me to help me get out of my situation.

On April 26, I finally worked enough nerve to contact Elaine for help; I wrote her the following letter:

Elaine,

Last week you left a message saying that you are not married. You also stated that your husband left and that you are awaiting his return.

But then you said it doesn't matter. Question: Does it matter or not?

I truly believe that things are not working out for me up here because I am out of position. I don't believe that this is where I should be. This is home but it doesn't feel like it. I felt much more at home when I was there. I thought I was doing the right thing moving back, but the right thing was staying there. There was another major reason I left besides my grandchild that I never told anyone. I was just too embarrassed and hurt.

I took the apartment in Gastonia expecting to share it with a friend who was moving from California. He had some personal (family) issues arise that required him to stay in California.

At that point I knew I couldn't afford the rent and had nowhere else to go, so I left.

I made a few mistakes while there. Being hard-headed and adamant about us (stupid) and then leaving. Now I'm paying dearly. Now that I've learned my mistakes and learned from my mistakes I can only hope and pray I can apply those things to the future.

Pray for me, I need it greatly as I need God to intervene (spelling) and straighten out the mess I've made. I was really happy there and I'm absolutely miserable here.

I want and need to come home and do the right thing and get married to the only person that showed me true unconditional love. I also need to stop putting conditions on myself, and just be myself. I need to stop letting the fear of failing rule me. I've walked away from two major blessings God bestowed on me.

It's too late for the Fire Dept. situation, but is it too late for us???

Love,

Robert

Elaine called me and stated that she would do everything possible to help me get back home, get a job, and get back on my feet.

I continued to work on getting the job with the bus company so that I would be able to earn enough money to get back to North Carolina, and the job finally came through.

I would only be working four hours a day but this would be better than nothing.

I kept in close contact with Elaine because I was determined that I was going to return to her and to North Carolina as soon as possible.

On May 10, I wrote another letter to Elaine.

Elaine,

I have not read this book as of yet, but I did watch T. D. Jakes on T.V. speaking and elaborating on major topics in the book & at the same some mime dancers were acting/dancing what T. D. was saying and I felt he was talking directly to me. I believe that you can help me achieve repositioning myself. There was a time that you held the desire of helping me reach my potential. I can only hope & pray that desire still exists within you.

I really want to return to you & to N.C. This is no longer home.

Returning will be financially difficult unless I wait until June. The cost of a rental truck, the car carrier, gas & tolls are a lot and I will probably have about $700.00 by June 22-23 saved up.

I also have an idea for a book/movie I really believe in. Talk soon.

Love,
Mr. Bob

Elaine and I continued to speak often regarding my returning to North Carolina. Elaine was faxing job applications to potential employers for me and placing applications online for me.

After taking the additional tests and getting the endorsements that I needed in Massachusetts to drive a school bus, I was finally able to get a part-time job around the first weeks in May. The job was temporary and was scheduled to last for about six weeks. The job did not offer any benefits and was only four hours per day.

Even though I was working, I was still not earning enough money to sustain myself. I was constantly getting advances off of my credit cards and I was getting deeper and deeper into debt.

On May 18, I received another blow to my life. My adoptive brother, Charles E. Richardson, affectionately called "Buster" and "Little Beaver," passed away. Charles's mother, Mrs. Helen Wilson Richardson, was the third person who kept me for a while when I was abandoned by my biological mother. Buster was six years older than me, but we were very close friends and I loved him like a brother. He had an older sister Claire who helped take care of me when I was present in the household. A younger sister Ethel was born later.

Buster had never married, but had a lifetime partner, Kathy Gallo. He also had seven daughters and two sons.

He had worked twenty-seven years and retired from the Worcester Standard Foundry.

Buster was a Native American, a member and Sub Chief of the Nipmuc Nation Indian Tribe. He was very active with the Grafton Reservation and spent many years operating the cook shack at the Annual Pow Wow Affair. He was also a longtime Harley

Davidson enthusiast and member of the Vietnam Veterans M/C
N.E. Club.

I was asked to sing a solo at Buster's funeral, which was held at
the Mt. Sinai Church of God in Christ, 63 Wellington Street,
Worcester, on Wednesday, May 23, 2007. I met with the family
and worked out all of the details, but I wasn't sure that I would
be able to make it through the service. I tend to get very emo-
tional at funerals and when I have to stand up alone before a large
crowd. I prayed that I would be able to make it through.

My job with the bus company ended around the middle of June
and I planned to leave for North Carolina on June 27.

I contacted Elaine and she made arrangements for a rental truck
and car hauler for me to make the move. I was to pick the truck
and car hauler up on Wednesday, June 27 between 7:00 and 8:00
a.m., and I advised Elaine that I would call her when I was loaded
and leaving Worcester.

By that time my friend and I were really not getting along at
all. She was aware that I was returning to North Carolina and
she probably knew that another woman was involved with my
move.

I had gotten ready to go pick up the guys who were to help me
load the truck when my friend and I got into an altercation over
money. She was refusing to permit me to remove my belongings
from the apartment unless I paid her $400. She felt that I owed
her at least that amount for the time that I had stayed there rent-
free, eaten her food, and shared other things. I tried to explain to
her that I didn't have but $600 and if I gave her $400, I would not
have enough money for gas and tolls to get to North Carolina. I
offered to send her money when I got settled in North Carolina

and started working, but she was adamant about my giving her the $400 now.

I asked her if it would be okay for me to take my music which was very valuable to me and leave the other items and furniture until I was able to send her the $400; she wouldn't budge.

The situation quickly escalated and finally got completely out of control and the police were called. I was very upset and I almost got arrested because I was refusing to leave the premises without my music. I was taken down to the police station but was released after I told my side of the story. Before being released I was given a court date to return for a hearing in the matter on Friday, July 13.

After everyone calmed down and I gave my friend the $400 that she was demanding, I was allowed to return to the residence and take my music and a few other personal belongings.

I called Elaine and advised her that I had cancelled the truck and that I would not be able to come to North Carolina. I advised her that I would have to stay in Worcester, because I didn't have enough money to move. I told Elaine part of the story, but I was not completely honest with her. I told her that I didn't want to talk about it right now, because I was too upset. I told her that we would discuss it later.

Elaine advised me to leave the property and come on to North Carolina. She stated that it was only property and that it could be replaced.

She also advised me that she had already scheduled four job interviews for me on the following week and stated that I really needed to keep the appointments. She also stated that I could go back to Worcester and pick up my belongings if necessary.

I advised her that I had only $200 and I didn't know if that would be enough to get me to North Carolina. Elaine, being the kind and caring person that she is, stated that she would come to meet me if I ran out of fuel before reaching home.

I didn't want to tell Elaine the truth about what had happened and why it had happened. All the way down the road I tried to come up with a story that would sound good, and I thought I had.

I arrived at Elaine's house in North Carolina around 5:00 p.m. on Sunday, July 1. When I arrived, I found that Elaine had a house guests, her sister Marie Padgett from Cleveland, Ohio and her brother Johnny Belcher from Anchorage, Alaska. They were eating dinner and asked me to join them. I declined the food and told Elaine that I wanted to visit with Aunt Janie for a short while and come back and go to bed, as I was exhausted from the trip.

When I returned from Aunt Janie's house, Marie and Johnny were leaving and had stopped at Elaine's mother's house to say hello. I did acknowledge that I saw them by tooting my car horn, but I deliberately did not stop to speak; I did not want to answer any questions.

I sat down with Elaine for a few minutes to tell her my story. I told her that I was staying with my friend John, who had two teenage sons who did not like my staying there and tried to get me into trouble. I told her about the altercation that we had and my version of how and why it took place. I also told her another story, my version, of the one I couldn't tell her over the telephone.

I was taking some herbs that I had gotten at the health food store to clean out my system from possible drugs. I told her that John's sons didn't like my staying at their father's place and they tried to mess up my license. They knew that I had my Class B Driver's License and they wanted me to lose my license. I told her that they would stand outside of my bedroom window while I was asleep during the day after my morning bus run and blow marijuana smoke through the window into my room. They were doing this in hopes that I would test positive for drug use if I had to take a random drug test on the job.

Elaine asked me, "What type of people are you dealing with that would do something like that to a friend?"

I told her that I thought that I knew these fellows, but I guessed I didn't. I never would have imagined that they would do anything like that to me. Of course I was lying; I knew exactly what was going on.

I had returned to my old environment in Worcester, with my old friends who were still using illegal drugs. I fell right back into the clique and resumed my old habits, and I knew exactly what I was doing. As usual, I was pretending to be someone that I was not and was blaming others for my bad choices.

My Cousin Carl Brooks came over and I learned that he and Elaine had gone into the farming business as partners. I rode over to the farm with Carl, and when I looked around at what they had accomplished, fear started to consume me again. Elaine and Carl would also go out every morning and pick fresh blackberries, which they sold.

It seemed that everything that Elaine touched turned into gold and she was constantly being blessed.

All the fear and anxiety that I had felt before started creeping back into my mind. How could I compete with Elaine? How could I feel like a man with her? Elaine had everything going for her, and

I had nothing. I just didn't think that I was going to be able to measure up to her because I knew that I wouldn't be able to keep up with her energy, and I just didn't feel like a man when I was around her.

Elaine showed me to my living quarters, which were separate from hers. I had my own private bedroom with a sitting area, private bathroom, kitchen, dining room, living room, and deck. I got unpacked and tried to settle down for the evening, but I was having a very difficult time relaxing. Fear was taking control of me and I didn't know how to handle it. I went downstairs to the kitchen and found a single beer in the refrigerator and I drank it. That helped me to calm down a little. I later found out that the beer can was a collector's item. I really didn't think about it at the time, but I was probably also withdrawing from substance abuse.

Elaine had set up four job interviews for me, two on Monday and two on Tuesday, July 2 and 3. I went for the interviews and was offered all four jobs. I decided to accept the job at the Bessemer City Middle School in Bessemer City, North Carolina.

The following day was the Fourth of July. Elaine's mother had a cookout, which we attended. Later that afternoon, I went to visit with my Aunt Janie and the rest of the family.

Later that evening, I told Elaine that I was going back to Worcester to pick up my belongings and say good-bye to my friends and that I would be back on Tuesday.

Elaine asked if she could go with me and help me to drive and I said no. She wanted to know why I was saying no, and I told her that I didn't want her to meet some of my friends because they were not very good people. The truth was I did not want her to see the condition that I was living in. I was very embarrassed with my situation. In essence, I was indigent and homeless.

On July 5, I was to leave for Worcester to pick up my clothes and the rest of my belongings (at least this was the story I told). Elaine suggested that I leave my car in North Carolina and rent a cargo van to pick up my belongings. This would reduce the cost of the trip substantially. I took her advice and we went to Gastonia to rent the cargo van for one week.

I left Thursday evening and arrived in Worcester on Friday morning. I spent the weekend resting, visiting friends, and thinking about how I was going to explain to Elaine that I was not going to be staying in North Carolina. I had made up my mind that I just couldn't handle the pressure and work required to live in the country. I was raised in the city and I didn't know how to keep up a house and a farm. I also had my upcoming court date on Friday the 13th and I did not know what the outcome would be.

I had told Elaine that I would be back on Tuesday the 10th, but I called her and told her that the boy who was supposed to help me move my furniture down from the third floor got tied up and couldn't come. I pretended to be very upset and told her that I had spoken with his parents and they had apologized for his not showing up, but stated that something came up and it couldn't be helped. I told her that I couldn't move the furniture down three flights of stairs by myself because it was 95 degrees that day. I told her that I would get loaded and leave out tomorrow.

Elaine reminded me that the cargo van had to be back in Gastonia by noon on Thursday and that I had an appointment on Thursday morning to get my drug screen for my job. The drug screen was another major concern for me. I wasn't sure that the herbs that

I had been taking had worked, and I didn't want to fail my drug test.

I left Worcester Wednesday night with an empty cargo van and arrived in North Carolina around 5:00 a.m. Thursday morning. I had made up my mind that I would not be staying in North Carolina. I went directly to bed and slept until Elaine woke me up around 9:15 a.m. Elaine asked me if I had missed my appointment and I was very evasive. I told her that I would be down in a few minutes. I stripped the bed and went to take a shower. My plan was to leave immediately with as little discussion as possible; I really didn't know what to say. I was just confused and frightened about everything; my mind was in a fog.

After about another forty-five minutes, Elaine came upstairs and called out to me. She stated that Belmont Middle School had called to offer me a job and they wanted me to call them back. Before I could get downstairs, the telephone rang again and it was the principal at Bessemer City Middle School, calling to see why I had not kept my appointment. I took the telephone and went upstairs where Elaine could not hear what I had to say. I told the principal that I would have to decline the position because I had to return to Massachusetts; of course, I didn't tell him the truth.

When I returned downstairs, Elaine asked me if I had rescheduled my appointment, and I said, "No, I have to return to Massachusetts."

She asked me, "When?" And I said to her, "Today."

Elaine just stood there and looked at me as though she was in shock. I told her that I had to be back in Worcester by 9:00 a.m. the next day. She asked me what had happened and if I was in some sort of trouble. She also asked me if I had to be in court by

9:00 a.m. on Friday. I told her yes, but stated that I was not in any trouble, but I had witnessed something that I wished that I had not seen and that I was the only witness. I was just in the wrong place at the wrong time. I did not have a choice, I had to return.

Elaine asked me when I would be returning to North Carolina, and I told her that I would write to her and after she reads the letter we would talk.

She asked, "What am I supposed to do?" And I replied, "Just keep busy as you always do."

I had completely forgotten that I had asked her to marry me again. It never occurred to me how hurt and upset she felt and I really didn't care. As usual, I was concentrating totally on me, my problems, and my feelings; nothing else really mattered.

On the way back from Gastonia to return the cargo van, Elaine and I had very little to say to one another. When we were almost home she finally asked if I was going to tell her the truth about what was going on, and I said that I didn't want to talk about it because I had been beat up on enough.

When we arrived back at home around noon, I went immediately to pack my belongings without a word to Elaine. Elaine went to her office to get some work done and was not aware that I was preparing to leave. When I finished packing, I took the keys down to her and said my good-byes.

I tried to hug Elaine, but she started to tremble, she flung her arms around, and pulled away from me. I was very hurt and upset, and I just walked out the door, leaving her standing there. Elaine came to the door and watched me drive away with tears in her eyes.

I made several calls to Elaine while on the road back to Worcester. It really hurt her that I had left the way I did, but I couldn't see any other way out.

I went to court the following morning, and my domestic disturbance case was heard and dismissed. I was relieved that that was finally behind me.

After I was finished in court I called Elaine to let her know that I was back in Worcester and that I had gotten the car unloaded and was going to bed. I told her that I was going to try to sleep for the next two days and that I would be in contact with her soon.

I tried to write to Elaine a few times and I tore the letters up three times. How do you write a letter to a woman who has been so kind and loving to you that you know will devastate her? I knew that I had to say something, even if it was another lie and excuse.

I finally settled on the following letter:

Writing this letter is extremely difficult. I've written and torn it up three times already. Hopefully this one will make it to the mail box.

First understand that I do love you. I love you enough to want the best for you, and I don't believe that is me. A good husband has the ability and does lead his family closer to God day by day. A good husband also provides and protects. My provisions are so limited I can't take care of myself. I live in a very ghetto-type life style and you knowing it is enough for me to deal with.

I need to be allowed the dignity of not having you see my situation. I am a sensitive person. There are times & ways I'm hurt very easily, when most people wouldn't be affected. I am who I am and my sensitivities are a part of my make-up, my identity. You have worked very hard and have sown sincerely and blessed others with what you've been blessed with. An observation of your faith and your acting on that faith.

I seem to continuously make wrong decisions. My faith isn't weak, but my ability to act on that faith is very weak even after watching others act on their faith and prosper, spiritually, financially, and in all areas of their lives.

You, with God's help & guidance have created a very warm & lovely living situation (home) for yourself. It's apparent how happy you are when one sees & observes you in your environment. As you know I was raised in the city and a northern city at that. As much as I like the country life, I know in my heart that I'm not cut out for that and find myself uncomfortable too often. I'm constantly looking for snakes & other animals that can pose a threat. 56 years on this earth and I can't even afford rent (what a man) and I'm being picky about where I live. But I'm being honest.

Here's another bit of honesty for you. I'm about $50,000 in debt. You helped me clear things (cards & debts) up and I turned around and messed them up again. Most of what I spent was for survival & some on stuff. Bottom line, I screwed up once again.

Another thing that matters to me is for me to see myself in the décor of the home I live in. It really helps one feel a part of that home.

You are a very pretty lady who carries herself with the utmost respect. At 56 I should be more settled by where I am. Still struggling with faith (acting on) and finances. You deserve someone who can compliment your life, not complicate it with their issues.

Love,

Robert

Elaine immediately wrote a five-page response to my letter and reassured me of her love for me and let me know that all of my fear is not of God. She again offered to help me in any way possible and let me know again that my financial situation does not matter to her. She feels that God is trying to use me and my talents and that Satan was trying to stop me from reaching my full potential.

Elaine reminded me of how she grew up in poverty and abuse and how God delivered and blessed her life. She sent me $25 to put minutes on my phone to call her because I had not called her as I promised after she had read my letter.

I was really avoiding calling Elaine; I didn't know how to respond to her letter. She is such a kind and loving person and I didn't want to continue to hurt her. I knew that my life was not what it should and could be, and I didn't know how to fix it.

Sunday morning August 19 at 8:57 a.m., I finally decided to call and leave a message for Elaine. I am such a coward; I waited until I knew that she would probably be in church before I called.

I left a message telling her that I had been sick since returning to Worcester, but for the past week I was feeling a little better. I told her that I had not been to the hospital or doctor, because as she already knew, I did not have medical insurance. I told her that I had not told Aunt Janie or Andre about my illness because I didn't want them to worry. I told her that I would be okay and that we would talk soon.

Elaine called and left a message that she had sent me some mail last week and she wanted to talk with me as soon as possible.

When I received the mail, it contained a sermon and book by Rev. Joel Osteen. The title of the CD was "Developing the Right

Anchor Thoughts" and the book was titled *Living a Fulfilled Life*. She also sent a letter letting me know that she had received my message and was sorry that I had not been feeling well and that she was happy to hear that I was feeling better. She sent me copies of two letters that I had written to her, and she underlined some important points. She also reminded me that I had promised to call her after she read my letter. She asked me if that was also another empty promise.

CHAPTER 9:
MY LIFE WAS A MESS

My life was in such a mess. I had gotten myself involved in a very bad situation and I didn't know how to resolve it. I tried everything that I knew to get my issues resolved but they just seemed to get worse. I always thought that I could take care of any situation but the people who I thought were my friends have turned their backs on me.

I decided to return to North Carolina one more time to try and get my life back on track. I knew that Elaine would be there for me and maybe I could reach my full potential with her.

I really felt guilty because I knew in my heart that I was not in love with Elaine, and I didn't think that I would be able to show her the love that she deserved. I would need to come up with some valid excuse to avoid being intimate with her, and I thought that I had the perfect answer.

I called Elaine the third Tuesday in September to let her know that I would be returning to North Carolina. I took the opportunity to tell her that I was not sexually adequate any longer. I told her that I thought that it might be related to my diabetes and health status. I also told her that I was no longer able to get any erection. She questioned me about this. She wanted to know who the lucky woman was. I told her that I was not involved with another woman, but that I had tried to masturbate and I could not get aroused or get an erection at all. Elaine asked me why I was telling her this, and I said that I was just making conversation.

She said that it was not necessary as we wouldn't be engaging in any sexual activities. She said, "Furthermore, sex is not the most important thing in a relationship especially at our age and with our health issues."

I was really relieved to hear her say that and it meant that neither one of us would be under any pressure.

Elaine advised me that she had already sent several job applications in for me. She was positive that I would get a job right away. Elaine had so much faith; I wish that I could have had half the faith that she had. I told her that I would call later in the week to give her my definite plans.

As Elaine had anticipated, I was offered a job with the Gaston County Schools right away. I advised the principal that I would need to give my current employer two weeks notice before I could start and he consented to wait on me.

Elaine was such a loving and kind woman, and I wished that I could have loved her, but I just didn't seem to have any feelings left for anything or anyone; not even myself. I felt numb and so distant from everyone and everything in the world.

I called Elaine back on Thursday, September 20, and advised her that I planned to leave Worcester on Wednesday, October 10. I anticipated arriving on the following afternoon.

I arrived at Elaine's house around 5:30 p.m. on Thursday afternoon. I was exhausted and advised her that I would wait until the next day to unload the truck. Elaine had my room ready and had made a delicious dinner for me. I felt so relieved to finally be in North Carolina again and was looking forward to starting work on Monday.

After I got settled and returned the truck, Elaine wanted to talk with me about what was going on. I told her that I didn't want to talk about it because it was over with and behind me. I just wanted to get on with my life. When she insisted, I told her that I had gotten involved with something that I wished that I had never gotten involved in. She wanted to know if I had broken the law, and I told her that it had nothing to do with the law. I asked her to forget about it because I didn't have any more to say; it was finished.

The truth was that I had made another bad decision. I had gotten involved with another woman because I needed a place to live and I had convinced the other woman that I wanted to make a life with her and I had gone so far as to ask her to marry me.

When this woman realized that I was not sincere about marrying her all hell broke loose. She let me know in no uncertain terms that I would not use her and just walk away without repaying her for what she had done for me. This woman was not one to play with and I didn't want Elaine to know what a louse I was.

I started my job as a custodian with the Gaston County Schools on Monday, October 15, and I was finally at peace. Elaine was always very kind and patient with me. She cooked every day, kept the house spotless, and gave me my privacy.

I was relieved that Elaine was not putting any pressure on me because I learned that my situation with the other woman had not been taken care of as I had thought. I was constantly on my cell phone trying to get the matter taken care of, but to no avail.

I was beginning to fall into a deeper depression and I think that Elaine noticed, but she did not say anything.

One afternoon I was watching a football game with my Cousin Carl Brooks when Elaine called me to her office and stated that I had a telephone call. I asked her who it was and she said, "It's a Mr. Ward." I answered the call and learned that it was my former friend Luther Ward from Worcester.

I was very upset because I didn't want to speak with Luther. I felt that he had terminated our friendship months ago. I was cordial to him and I asked him how he had gotten Elaine's telephone number, and he said that he went on the Internet under People Search USA and located me. I did not believe Luther because I felt that he did not care enough for me that he would pay to locate me.

After my conversation with Luther, I confronted Elaine and she said that she didn't know how Luther had gotten her unlisted telephone number, but that she was familiar with People Search USA. I didn't believe her and I told her that she had really overstepped her bounds and that she was to leave my personal relationships to me to handle.

Elaine said that I should have been happy to hear from my friend, but I told her that he was no longer my friend. She asked me what had happened, and I told her that Luther had done something to me that broke up our friendship. Elaine wanted to know what could have possibly happened to break up such a close long-term friendship, but I didn't want to elaborate any further on the subject; I just wanted to forget my former friend.

Elaine, being the peacemaker that she was, suggested that I talk to Luther about my feelings and try to fix whatever the problem was. She said that it was important for me to talk to Luther honestly, forgive him, and then let go. I told her that it was up to Luther to fix the problem because he had created it. I told Elaine that I had spoken with Luther's mother at church one Sunday, and the conversation basically confirmed what I thought had happened and there was no need for me to contact Luther.

I told Elaine whatever she had done on the Internet to make it possible to locate me, to get rid of it now. I repeated this to her several times that evening; I didn't want to be located by anyone.

A few weeks after my arrival in North Carolina, to my utter surprise, my friends Harry and Lenny Johnson called and advised me that they were going to Roanoke, Virginia, to visit a friend and wanted to stop by to see me since they would be so close. They wanted to take their last fall trip in Harry's convertible before he garaged it for the winter.

I told the guys that I was very busy and would have little time to see them, and I thought that they would not come. However, on Wednesday morning, November 7, I received a call from Harry stating that they were in Kings Mountain. Boy was I surprised.

I had a doctor's appointment in Gastonia that afternoon, so I asked them to meet me at the mall and we could have lunch together. I referred them to the Holiday Inn Express in Kings Mountain to sleep over. I called Elaine when I got to work to let her know that they were in town and that I would be stopping by the hotel after work to spend some time with them. She did not answer the telephone, but I left a message for her.

When I got off from work, I picked up my messages and found that Elaine had called and told me to bring my friends to her house to stay. I went by the hotel and told the guys that I would pick them up in the morning.

Elaine was up when I arrived home, but she did not come out of her room to speak with me; she had written a note to me that was on the kitchen counter.

The note read: "Robert, please invite your friends to stay at our home. It would be ashamed to have them travel such a long distance to see you and permit them to stay in a hotel. They are welcome to stay at the house."

The next morning I asked Elaine where were Harry and Lenny supposed to sleep and she said, "One in my room, one in your room, or on the daybed in the office." I didn't want her to give up her room, but she insisted that it was okay for us guys to have the house downstairs and that she would sleep upstairs.

Everything worked out real well. Elaine cooked for the guys and entertained them while I was at work; the guys really liked Elaine.

My peace was short-lived and my past was again catching up with me. I thought that I had taken care of my issues with the other woman before leaving Massachusetts, but it was obvious that I was wrong. Again I tried to take care of the problem by telephone, but the problem simply escalated. I had to make a decision right away as the situation was getting out of hand and I didn't want Elaine to find out the truth.

On Tuesday, November 13, I decided that I had to tell Elaine that I was leaving. She was busy working on the computer when I approached her and asked her a question. I asked, "Elaine, can I get you to do me a favor?"

She asked, "What is it?"

I asked, "Can I leave my things here until I can return and pick them up?"

Elaine looked up at me in total disbelief and asked me what I was talking about. I told her that I had to return to Massachusetts right away and that I would not return to live in North Carolina ever again. I told her that I would return with a truck around April to pick up the rest of my belongings. I could tell that Elaine was stunned, and I hated to do this to her, but again I felt that I had no choice.

Elaine wanted to know what was going on this time; I told her that I didn't want to talk about it; I just had to leave. Elaine tried to get me to talk, but I couldn't. She insisted and stated that I could not take the car if I could not tell her what was going on. She asked about my job and I told her that I would not be returning to North Carolina.

I said, "I am sick and tired of running up and down the road; I am just going to stay in Worcester. I will get a truck and return to pick up the rest of my things in April."

I told her that I planned to leave on Friday, but if I couldn't take the car, I would have to leave right away because I would have to take the bus or something.

Elaine insisted that I give her more information and I told her that I had to be back by Monday, otherwise all hell would break loose and I might be killed. I said, "It will be bad, believe me, and the less you know the better off you will be; trust me."

Elaine wanted to know what I had done, and I told her that I didn't do anything; I was just in the wrong place at the wrong time.

I went to work the next day and gave my two-day notice. My employer was very disappointed, but I explained that I thought the situation had been taken care of; otherwise, I would not have come down at the time.

I spent the next two days getting what little I could take with me in the car and I planned to leave early Friday morning.

Elaine waited up for me Thursday evening and tried to talk with me again, but I had nothing more to say. I told her that I didn't want her to be in the middle of a mess. She said that no one knew where I was, so I would be safe here. I explained to her that the men knew where I was and she could get hurt and that was why I could not give her any more details.

Elaine kept insisting that I talk, so to get her to stop, I made up another lie. I pretended to get very emotionally upset and I started to cry. I said, "Elaine, you don't understand what is going on with my health. I have tuberculosis and I shouldn't be around you; I could make you sick because you have such a fragile immune system. Let me go and take care of this business and try to address my health problems. I don't want to be a burden on you."

Elaine said, "Okay Robert, I won't ask you any more questions; do what you must."

At that point she walked out of the room and went to her office to work on her computer.

When I was ready to leave on Friday, Elaine gave me food and medicine and wished me well. I didn't know what to say. She hugged me and I said, "No tears, please." I then said, "I will tell you this. One night on my way home from Shrewsbury, on Highway 9, I picked up two guys that I knew and they had done something which I was not aware of. Some people were looking for them and when they caught up with them, they were in the car with me. The men thought that I had something to do with what had happened, but I didn't know anything about it. Even though the guys told the men that I wasn't involved, they did not believe them, so I have to go back and take care of this matter."

Surprisingly, Elaine's reaction was completely different from the previous times when I left. This time she was very upbeat; she wished me well and said that she would be praying for me.

I couldn't exactly put my hands on it, but she didn't appear to be upset at all. She hugged me and gave me a big smile when I was ready to leave and she said, "Robert, please take care of yourself; God bless you."

I arrived back in Worcester Saturday morning around 11:50 a.m. I was extremely tired from the trip as I was not able to relax at all in the overloaded car. I called and left a message for Elaine around 11:56 a.m. letting her know that I had arrived back in Worcester safe and sound, but she did not answerer the telephone.

I got the car unloaded and tried to take a nap, but couldn't sleep; I think that I was too tired from the long drive.

I called Elaine again around 4:30 p.m. She answered the telephone this time and I told her that I was safe, but very tired. I told her that I had forgotten my cereal bowls and that I was upset when I couldn't have a bowl of cereal. She offered to mail the bowls to me, but I told her no because they only cost a dollar.

Elaine asked me where I was staying and I told her with the same guys at the half-way house. I was careful not to give her an address. She asked why I didn't borrow a bowl from one of them, and I told her that they didn't have one, they were drug addicts. I then quickly said, "Recovering drug addicts." I told her that I was going to try and take a nap because I was very tired and that I would call her later.

I called again on Thanksgiving morning to wish Elaine a Happy Thanksgiving Day. She asked me where I was spending the day and I told her here at the house watching the games. She asked me why I wasn't spending the day with my friends and I told her that I had called Harry to let him know that I was back, but no invitation was extended. I told Elaine that over the years, I had gotten accustomed to being alone and that I would be okay. Elaine said that she was sending out Thanksgiving prayers by e-mail to family and friends and since I didn't have e-mail she would say the prayer to me. She said that she wished that she could send me Thanksgiving dinner over the airways.

I told Elaine that I was scheduled to start work driving a school bus with my former employer on Monday, but they had changed the start date to Tuesday. I advised her that I would resume making my monthly payments again as soon as I started getting paid.

Elaine responded by saying, "God bless you and have a Happy Thanksgiving Day."

I said, "You too."

We hung up the telephone without any further comments.

I then called Aunt Janie and the family to let them know that I was back in Worcester and to wish them a Happy Thanksgiving. Needless to say, they were also shocked at my move back to Massachusetts.

I spoke mostly to Aunt Janie and Andre, but everyone wanted to know what was going on. As usual, I just tried to make light of the situation. I told Aunt Janie that I had made my final move and that I would not be returning to North Carolina to live; I am tired and I will stay put this time.

I had been working and trying to take care of my business, but things were still not going well for me. Everyone appeared to be so distant, even Elaine, the one person that I had always been able to count on. I called Elaine and she did not respond immediately to my calls, but she was still kind to me.

A few days ago I received a box with my mail and several boxes of herbal teas from her, and I was happy to get it. I called to thank her, but she did not answer the telephone. I left a message, which she did not return. It is very unusual for Elaine not to return a telephone call so I called and left a second message. I thought maybe the message did not register or something had happened. Elaine again did not respond to my second call. I tried once more and she answered the telephone. She was very cool and stated that she had gotten my messages and hoped that I was doing well. I really didn't hear the usual excitement in her voice; it was like speaking to a stranger. I guess that I had finally managed to disappointment one of the best friends that I have ever had. The conversation was very short and she did not seem to have very much to say.

I just couldn't seem to escape problems and trouble no matter where I went or what I did. I hadn't even worked a good month when the weather turned out to be really bad. We had heavy snow and ice, and this meant that the schools were closed and I was out of work again. I was hoping to get a part-time job, but I hadn't been able to get my schedule worked out with the bus company.

The Christmas holidays were fast approaching and I felt a little sad. I was hoping to be finally settled in my life by now but I just couldn't seem to stop messing up. "MESS UP" should be my name, as this is what I did best. Yes, I am feeling sorry for myself; I knew that I had made a mess for myself.

I haven't heard from Elaine lately and I wonder how she is doing. I never thought that I would or could miss her as much as I did. I sent her a Christmas card and a $30 money order for my AAA membership payment. I wrote, "Love, Robert" on the card, then I realized that maybe I shouldn't continue to lie to her.

I wrote over "love" and wrote, "Loving friend, Robert."

I don't even know what I feel any more: love, hate, indifference, and fear; who knows? Certainly not me.

I received a Christmas card from Elaine. I guess that Elaine was also thinking about me because our cards crossed in the mail. This was the first time that she did not sign her card with love. I guess I was finally getting what I wanted: being alone.

Elaine had told me that she was going to spend some time with her sisters and sister-in-law in Ohio during the Christmas holiday and I wondered if she was already there. I wanted to call her, but I just didn't know what to say. And since I hadn't started back making my monthly payments to her, I really felt embarrassed.

It was four more days till Christmas and then a New Year; it was hard to believe that I still hadn't made any progress. I promised myself that I would do my best to make the New Year a better year and try to get to where I needed to be.

I guessed that it would be difficult for me to succeed if I couldn't admit why I had always been a failure. I had spent all my life trying to take advantage of others, instead of going out and making it on my own. It did not help for my parents to spoil me rotten, because I grew up believing that I was entitled. Not only was I entitled, I had to have everything my way; I had to be in full control of every situation.

One of the biggest hurdles in my life had always been how to deal with my sexuality. I had always wanted to be a man like the father who raised me but that didn't happen. God did not endow me as well as some other men, and I have always felt a little self-conscious and inadequate as a man. Women would say that it didn't matter, but it always became an issue later on in the relationship, and it didn't take long. I reached the point that I was reluctant to get involved in any intimate relationship because it was too painful when it ended.

I was frequently called a faggot by my female partners, and that hurt me deeply. I was very sensitive and I would cry easily when hurt, but I didn't think that crying made me less of a man. My mother always taught me that homosexuality was an abomination under God and that I should fear God and his wrath.

My life had been so turbulent and confusing that I sometimes didn't know what to think or believe.

I have always said, "I came into this world alone and I will die in this world alone."

Another issue was my inability to forgive the people that I felt had wronged me.

I had one real chance to change my outcome, but I let my PRIDE and inability to love mess it up. I had a beautiful Christian woman who loved me very much and offered me everything that she had, but I couldn't let go of the past and my anger.

I had always said that I wanted someone to love me unconditionally and never let me go, but when I found that person, I didn't know how to love her back. I saw her as a threat or something; she was so much like my mother. I knew that she loved me very much and was trying to do everything possible to make me happy, but my past would not let her in.

Christmastime and I was still alone. The holidays were the worst; that was when I really missed having my own family. Last Christmas I was in North Carolina with Aunt Janie and the family and I was very happy. I knew that I couldn't get that back, but I wished that I could.

I called Elaine to wish her a Merry Christmas, but she did not answer the telephone. I guess she was having breakfast with her mother or she could have been in Ohio or Alaska.

I called Aunt Janie and the entire family was there. Carnell, her husband, and Prince were there from Philadelphia, Pennsylvania. Lillian and her husband were there from Florida and family members were there from everywhere. I spent hours on the telephone speaking with everyone, and it really made me feel good to talk with them.

Andre and I spoke and he wanted to know how I was really doing and I told him that I was fine and that I was working and looking forward to getting another job at the Boys Club. I hadn't been able to get the job at the Boys Club because my hours with the bus company were not settled as yet.

CHAPTER 10:
JUST DRIFTING

Months passed and nothing changed in my life. I remained in the same poor position that I was in when I returned to Massachusetts. I have called on Elaine to help me with my medicine several times and she has always come through for me, but the relationship is not the same.

I was not happy being back in Massachusetts but I had no other place to go and I did not know what else I could do.

I had a friend living in Worcester who was planning to return home to Houston, Texas and he invited me to move down to Houston with him. He stated that I could live with him until I got a job and got settled. My friend also stated that the employment opportunities were good in Houston and that he would help me to get a job. I thought about it for awhile, but I wasn't sure that it was the right thing to do at the time.

Instead of moving to Texas I chose to return to my previous job driving a school bus. I also continued to look for a part time job to help supplement my income.

It wasn't long before things started to go wrong on my school bus driving job, and I no longer liked what I was doing. The children were very hard-headed and unruly on the bus, and they did not like to be corrected.

Again, operating solely on emotions, I decided that I would just quit my school bus driving job and move to Texas with my friend. I was hoping that I would be able to find a job in Houston that would be full-time with benefits and pay more than I was currently earning in Worcester.

I contacted my friend who had already moved back to Houston and advised him that I had reconsidered and that I would be taking him up on his offer. I relocated to Houston at the beginning of April.

A week before moving to Texas, I had called Elaine and asked her to help me again with my medicine as I had almost completely run out.

Elaine asked me again where I was living and who the contact person would be in case there was an emergency with me. I sort of hesitated answering her because I didn't want her to know that I was moving to Texas.

Instead of being upfront and honest with her, and letting her know that I was moving, I just gave her the address where I was moving from.

I stated that I lived at #23 Burke Street in Worcester and that the emergency contact person would be Harry. I also gave her Harry's telephone number in case she needed to call. I did not know it at the time, but Elaine already had the #23 Burke Street address and was already suspicious about my whereabouts.

Again I had to ask Elaine for help in getting my medicine. She asked me what was the status of my Massachusetts Medical Application and I told her that it was still being processed. I said, "You know how the government works; they just take their time, but if I should get sick they will take care of me; I just don't have my prescription coverage yet."

Elaine sent the medicine as I had requested to my post office box in Worcester and requested "Delivery Confirmation." I had placed a forwarding order with the post office in Worcester before I left for Texas and the package was forwarded to the post office there.

About two weeks later Elaine had left a message on my cell phone for me to call and let her know if I had received the package; I ignored her call because I didn't want to speak with her in case she had more questions for me.

I finally got up enough nerve to call Elaine on Mother's Day to thank her for the medicine and to wish her a Happy Mother's Day. Elaine did not appear to be her usual happy and upbeat self, and I asked her what was wrong and she replied that she was having a difficult time with her allergies. She did not talk very much and hurried off of the telephone; this was not the same Elaine that I was accustomed to speaking with.

I also called Aunt Janie and her daughters to wish them a Happy Mother's Day. As usual all of the family was there and they were having a ball. Every holiday is a major celebration at Aunt Janie's house. Oh how I longed to be there in the midst of such a close-knit and happy family.

I soon learned why Elaine had been so cool towards me. She had sent me a certified letter around the second week in May but I did not accept it. I was sure that she was demanding the return of the car that she had assisted me in purchasing. I was in default for about nine months at the time. She probably knew that I had lied about the whereabouts of the car and she was attempting to repossess it. I didn't know how I was going to work this out, but I knew that I didn't want to return the car; I needed it to look for work.

Once again my lies had caught up with me and I had created yet another mess for myself. Oh well, I would just have to appeal to the Christianity in her in order to buy more time. I also needed to figure out a way to get my belongings that I left at her house without giving her the car.

Elaine was scheduled to leave for her vacation on May 12 so I decided to call her house and leave a message for her, letting her know that I had not forgotten my debt. To my surprise Elaine answered the telephone and I had no choice but to tell her that I was not working since I had not made my regular monthly payments.

I told Elaine that I thought that she was on her cruise and she said, "It's not until the 17th." I said, "Oh, I'm confused, I thought that today was the 17th; I've just gotten my days and time all mixed up."

I had to come up quickly with another story to tell her to justify my not paying. I said, "Elaine, I am not working at the present time; I got fired from my bus driving job. I mean, I got suspended, but I am not going back. The kids on the school bus were throwing paper out of the windows and when I ordered them to stop they started threatening me. I told the kids that they were not going to do anything to me because I wasn't going to be bullied by a bunch of kids.

The children reported to the bus service that I had threatened them and I was called into the office. I was given an ultimatum to take anger management classes or be terminated and was placed on suspension until I enrolled in the classes. I do not have an anger management problem, and I refuse to let a bunch of kids intimidate me; so I quit the job. I am in the process of looking for another job and I will resume my payments as soon as I start back to work."

Elaine did not respond to what I had said; she just said, "I wish you the best and I will be praying for you." I have called Elaine, but she does not answer the telephone; I guess that she is on vacation. I had a job interview a few days ago and I called her while I was waiting to go in for my interview. I wanted her prayers for favor in getting the job but she did not answer the telephone.

I didn't know what the future would hold for me; I didn't even know if I would have a future; I would just keep on doing what I must do to survive as long as I can.

I finally found a job working with iron and steel. The job was extremely difficult and the Texas climate was very hot.

I did not like it in Houston at all; the city was too large and congested with traffic. With my lack of sense of direction, I was always making the wrong turn and getting lost.

The weather was absolutely too hot for me. I normally sweat and the heat there was almost unbearable.

I had to work a ten-hour shift each day and four hours on Saturday. My work schedule required me to get up at 2:00 a.m. in order to be on the job by 4:00 a.m., and it had been very difficult for me to make the adjustment. The job was very hard physical labor and

I was extremely exhausted when I got off from work; I usually went directly home and to bed.

Another issue which I faced was that I felt as though I was working in Mexico. Almost everyone on the job was from Mexico and they spoke Mexican on the job. It was several weeks before I saw a person of another race in the area where I lived and that made me feel better.

I picked up my voice mail messages and I had a message from Elaine asking me to call her. I really didn't want to have a conversation with her because I hadn't kept up with my obligations; I thought that I would just wait awhile before calling her back.

A few days later my Cousin Andre called and left a message for me to call Elaine because it was urgent that she speak with me right away.

The next day I called Elaine, and as I had imagined the news was not good. Elaine was very displeased with me and let me know in no uncertain terms that she was tired of dealing with me. She stated that she was extremely disappointed with my actions and called me a pathetic liar. She also advised me that she knew that I was in Texas and that she did not appreciate my lying to her when she asked me where the car was.

I tried to explain to her that I had not lied when I spoke with her; I told her that my plans were made on the spur of the moment. If I thought that that statement was going to make a difference, I was sadly mistaken. Elaine flew into me like a mad hornet and I failed at trying to defend myself.

I had to tell her that I had to hang up because my Tracfone was running out of minutes and I had to go to the store to recharge it, otherwise it would be no good. I stated, "Elaine, I will call you back in a few minutes; just let me go to recharge the phone."

After hanging up the phone, I rushed to the store to get my Tracfone recharged. I called Elaine from the store but the call went directly to her voice mail; she must have received another call.

When I arrived back at the house I called her again and she resumed her well-deserved pounding on me. She wanted to know why I had not called her to inform her as to the whereabouts of the car and I told her that I had called Harry to let him know that I was in Texas and that he would be the emergency contact person.

Elaine stated, "Robert, you are such a liar; I have spoken with Harry and he does not know where you are and it is not his responsibility to keep up with you. Harry or no one else needs to be involved in your mess. You are a grown man and you need to take care of your business."

I insisted that I had not lied and that Harry would be contacted if something happened to me. Elaine said, "Robert, as long as you are not sick, injured, or dead, you need to be the one to contact me. You don't owe Harry the money; you owe me and you need to show me some respect."

I was getting nowhere fast; I'd never heard Elaine speak so boldly; I was shocked.

She continued, "Robert, you put yourself in my place for just one moment, if that's possible. How would you feel if the shoe was on the other foot, but of course, I know that you would have never done the same for me?"

I finally insisted that she listen to me and let me explain what had really taken place. I told her that some friends had invited me to come down to Texas and they offered to help me get a job. The trip was paid for by the company that I would be working for and all I had to do was to get to Texas. I told her that I did not intend to remain in Texas because I would be returning to my bus driving job in Massachusetts.

I told her how I had gotten lost several times trying to get to Texas and how I had left my tooth at a motel where I spent the night and did not realize it until I was several hundred miles away. I told her that I went to Texas out of necessity, not out of desire.

Elaine listened patiently until I had told my story and then she let me have it again with both barrels. She said, "Robert, you need to stop lying. You did not get to Texas free; no gas station is going to let you pump gas for free and no motel is going to give you free room and board. When are you going to grow up and start thinking things through before you jump up and make a move; haven't you made enough bad decisions? You have absolutely no respect for me as a person or even as a friend. I am tired of dealing with you and I don't plan to spend the next ten years trying to keep up with you. I want to end this charade right now because it was just a lie from the very beginning."

I said, "Elaine, how can you say that I am not your friend and that I don't respect you after all that you have done for me? I may not respond to you in the way that you want me to, but I do respect you a great deal and you have been one of the best friends that I have ever had. I am sorry that I don't know how to express myself in a way that you would understand how I really feel about you."

I then asked her if she was going to take the car back and she said, "I don't even want to see the car because it would only remind me of a very disturbing and tragic period in my life that should not have even taken place."

I asked her to please permit me to keep the car because I liked it and I needed it for work.

I stated that I would send her a payment on Friday when I got paid and I told her that she was and would always be at the top of the list when I paid my bills.

Elaine said, "I am too upset to even continue this discussion; call me back after I return from my vacation and I will let you know what must be done."

She said, "I'm done, I'm too done with this." She then asked me for my street address in Texas and she wanted to know why I had not picked up my certified mail at the post office in Texas. I told her that I was not aware of any mail being at the post office; I had not received a notice. She just breathed hard and said, "Give me the address and I will talk with you later."

I gave her the address because I realized that she already had it and was giving me another "Liar Test."

Busted! Busted! I'm busted! I knew that I couldn't hide from that woman; why did I even try? After watching her work on her computer and tracking down my birth record that I didn't even know existed, I knew that I could not go anywhere in this world and not have her find me; not even the cemetery, but I tried.

I'm just drifting from one bad situation into another. Soon I'll be on the road again going back to I don't know where. What's wrong with me? Will I ever have any peace in my life? God help me, please!

EPILOGUE: "No Ending"

Robert's Story Continues:

There are still so many unanswered questions. Who is the real Robert Edward Johnston? What is he really like deep down inside of his soul? How does one discern what is the truth and what are lies?

Robert had not confronted and dealt with the numerous issues that have affected his ability to love and succeed in life.

He also has not completed the process to have his name legally changed to Robert Edward Johnston. Based on the Record of Birth, which was recorded in 1974, Robert was legally Harold Felix Saucier.

After listening to and writing Robert's story, it occurred to me that he is not really the person that I thought he was; I don't mean this in a negative way. I have seen several different personalities in this one complex man over the three-year period in which I was involved with him.

It occurred to me that just maybe some of Robert's problems were due to medical or psychological issues rather than just being malicious. I had seen the child, the man, and the monster, and I grieve for them all.

Since childhood Robert had problems with authority, discipline, and the inability to focus his attention. And additionally he had abused alcohol and drugs since his adolescent and early teenage years.

I started to ask myself some questions that I was not been able to answer; my single desire is to know the real truth.

First, where does Robert's story end? I knew the beginning and I knew the middle, but I did not know where or how his story would end.

Second, my question is, "Will Robert ever find peace and true happiness in his life or is he destined to continue drifting from one negative situation into another?"

I saw Robert as several different people with so many different personalities.

The person that I initially met was such a gentle, kind, and caring man, and I cannot forget that person, for he touched my heart in so many ways. I believed that some where deep down inside of him that person was still hidden and was struggling to get out.

The Robert that I knew was a man of God who knew what he wanted out of life and was willing to 'bend to fit.' He was a sensitive man who had endured a lot of hurt and pain, but he had survived. He was also a very outgoing man with a charming personality.

Everyone who met him was thoroughly impressed by his charisma and captivating personality. He communicated well with everyone and appeared to be open and honest.

Robert had so many special talents; if only he would have used them in a positive way. He was an excellent singer, voice teacher, poetry writer, and mentor, and he had several other positive attributes.

After several months had passed, suddenly without any prior warning, a new personality started to emerge. The new person was introverted; he did not have very much to say to anyone. He was starting to withdraw and appeared to be disenchanted with life. I noticed that he was no longer engaging people in conversation. Robert would sit back, watch and listen to people talk, and then he would make his own assessment of their character and intentions.

Robert was becoming extremely judgmental of people and voiced distrust and suspicions regarding the motives of certain individuals. He also appeared to have an exaggerated sense of his own importance. He indicated on more than one occasion that people born and raised in the city had more intelligence than people born and raised in the country.

Finally the stranger emerged. This was a person that I did not know at all, and I did not particularly care for this person due to his negative attitude. This person was an angry man who was filled with hatred and lacked forgiveness. He exhibited unusual characteristics; this man felt unloved and persecuted by everyone.

Robert was very unhappy and was withdrawing from all of the people who loved him the most.

I had not given up on Robert, but I was exhausted by the constant turmoil that he continued to bring into his life. I continued to be a friend and cared about his future and well-being, but I felt that it was time for me to move on.

I prayed that by telling Robert's story he would receive the help that he so desperately needed to defeat the demons that continued to haunt him.

Hopefully by reading his own story, Robert was able to see the many blessings that he has been afforded in life, and that it would help bring some closure to his traumatic beginning.

ABOUT THE AUTHOR

Doris Elaine Smarr was born on January 22, 1948, in Bessemer City, North Carolina, and raised by her grandparents, Anderson and Minnie House Smarr, on a farm in Kings Mountain, North Carolina, where she had a humble beginning.

"Elaine," as she prefers to be called, has always enjoyed writing and previously wrote several poems, speeches, and short stories as a teenager, which were never published. She has now decided that

it is time to fulfill one of her many dreams: one of which was to become a writer.

After graduating from Compact High School in Kings Mountain in June 1965, Elaine relocated to New York City, where she attended and graduated from the Market Training Institute in 1967and the New York Business School in 1969. She also studied the Italian language at Hunter College of New York.

She then married and relocated to Italy in 1969.

After her divorce Elaine returned to the United States and continued to pursue her education at the Gaston College in Dallas, NC.

Elaine graduated with honors from Gaston College in 1988, where she received an Associate of Arts degree.

Elaine is the mother of two sons: Kenny and Christian Ollemi (deceased). She is also a grandmother and great-grandmother.

She is a member of the National Association for Female Executives and is a lifetime Girl Scout.

Elaine is a dedicated member of the St. Peter Missionary Baptist Church in Grover, North Carolina, where she volunteers in the office as a financial clerk and is also a member of the Hymn and Mass Choirs, Prison Ministry, Nursing Home Ministry, and Visitors Telephone Ministry.

Beabo is the first of many books she has planned to write. She is currently in the process of writing two other books. Due to her love for family history, she plans to write her life story and that of her closest friends in the near future.

Printed in the United States
132603LV00003B/4/P